Bob Dylan
The Illustrated Record

BOB DYLAN

THE ILLUSTRATED RECORD

by Alan Rinzler

Designed by Jon Goodchild

Harmony Books / New York

Inquiries should be addressed to:
Harmony Books
a division of Crown Publishers, Inc.
One Park Avenue, New York,
New York 10016

Published simultaneously in Canada by General Publishing Co., Ltd. Printed in the United States of America

First Printing

Library of Congress Cataloging in Publication Data:

Rinzler, Alan.
Bob Dylan : the illustrated record.

1. Dylan, Bob, 1941-
2. Singers—United States—Biography. I. Goodchild, Jon.
ML420.D98R56 784'.092'4 78-7006
ISBN 0-517-533545
ISBN 0-517-533553 (pbk.)

Book Design: Jon Goodchild
Book title lettering: Jim Parkinson
Typeset by Jomiratype, San Francisco

Front cover photograph: Len Siegler
Title page photograph: George Gruel
Opposite: © 1967 Daniel Kramer

The photographs on pages 5, 26, 29, 37 are from the book entitled "Bob Dylan," © 1967 by Daniel Kramer, published by Citadel Press, permission granted by the author.

Acknowledgments

The following song is copyright by Duchess Music Corp: Song to Woody, © 1962.

The following songs are copyright by M. Witmark & Sons: Hard Rain, © 1963; Don't Think Twice, © 1963; Talking World War III Blues, © 1963; Honey, Just Allow Me One More Chance, © 1963; I Shall Be Free, © 1963; Times They Are A-Changin', © 1963; With God On Our Side, © 1963; Only a Pawn in Their Game, © 1963; When the Ship Comes In, © 1963; The Lonesome Death of Hattie Carroll, © 1964; Restless Farewell, © 1964; All I Really Want To Do, © 1964; Spanish Harlem Incident, © 1964; My Back Pages, © 1964; I Don't Believe You, © 1964; Ballad in Plain D, © 1964; It Ain't Me Babe, © 1964; Subterranean Homesick Blues, © 1965; Maggie's Farm, © 1965; Mr. Tambourine Man, © 1964; Gates of Eden, © 1965; It's Alright, Ma (I'm Only Bleeding), © 1965, 1966; It's All Over Now, Baby Blue, © 1965; Like A Rolling Stone, © 1965; Tombstone Blues, © 1965; It Takes a Lot to Laugh, It Takes a Train to Cry, © 1965; Ballad of a Thin Man, © 1965; Queen Jane Approximately, © 1965; Just Like Tom Thumb's Blues, © 1965; Tomorrow Is A Long Time, © 1963.

The following songs are copyright by Dwarf Music: Rainy Day Women #12 & 35, © 1966, 1976; Pledging My Time, © 1966, 1976; One of Us Must Know (Sooner or Later), © 1966, 1976; I Want You, © 1966, 1976; Stuck Inside of Mobile With the Memphis Blues Again, © 1966, 1976; Leopard-Skin Pill-Box Hat, © 1966, 1976; Just Like a Woman, © 1966, 1976; Fourth Time Around, © 1966, 1976; Sad-Eyed Lady of the Lowlands, © 1966, 1976; John Wesley Harding, © 1968, 1976; As I Went Out One Morning © 1968, 1976; I Dreamed I Saw St. Augustine, © 1968, 1976; All Along the Watchtower, © 1968, 1976; The Ballad of Frankie Lee and Judas Priest, © 1968, 1976; Dear Landlord, © 1968, 1976; I Am a Lonesome Hobo, © 1968, 1976; I Pity the Poor Immigrant, © 1968, 1976; The Wicked Messenger, © 1968, 1976; Down Along the Cove, © 1968, 1976; I'll Be Your Baby Tonight, © 1968, 1976; The Mighty Quinn, © 1968, 1976; I Shall Be Released, © 1967, 1976; You Ain't Goin' Nowhere, © 1967, 1976.

The following songs are copyright by Big Sky Music: To Be Alone With You, © 1969, 1976; I Threw It All Away, © 1969, 1976; Peggy Day, © 1969, 1976; Lay, Lady, Lay, © 1969, 1976; Tell Me That It Isn't True, © 1969, 1976; All the Tired Horses, © 1970, 1976; If Not For You, © 1970, 1976; Day of the Locusts, © 1970, 1976; Time Passes Slowly, © 1970, 1976; Went to See the Gypsy, © 1970, 1976; Winterlude, © 1970, 1976; If Dogs Run Free, © 1970, 1976; New Morning, © 1970, 1976; Sign on the Window, © 1970, 1976; One More Weekend, © 1970, 1976; The Man in Me, © 1970, 1976; Three Angels, © 1970, 1976; Father of Night, © 1970, 1976; Watching the Rivers Flow, © 1971, 1976; When I Paint My Masterpiece, © 1971, 1976.

The following songs are copyright by Ram's Horn Music: Billy, © 1972, 1976; Knockin' On Heaven's Door, © 1973, 1976; On a Night Like This, © 1973, 1976; Going, Going, Gone, © 1973, 1976; Tough Mama, © 1973, 1976; Something There Is About You, © 1973, 1976; Forever Young, © 1973, 1976; Dirge, © 1973, 1976; Never Say Goodbye, © 1973, 1976; Wedding Song, © 1974, 1976; Tangled Up in Blue, © 1974, 1976; Simple Twist of Fate, © 1974, 1976; You're a Big Girl Now, © 1974, 1976; Idiot Wind, © 1974, 1976; You're Gonna Make Me Lonesome When You Go, © 1974, 1976; If You See Her Say Hello, © 1974, 1976; Shelter From the Storm, © 1974, 1976; Buckets of Rain, © 1974, 1976; Hurricane, © 1975; Isis, © 1975, 1976; Mozambique, © 1975, 1976; One More Cup of Coffee, © 1975, 1976; Oh, Sister, © 1975, 1976; Joey, © 1975, 1976; Black Diamond Bay, © 1975, 1976; Sara, © 1975, 1976.

The following are copyright by Bob Dylan: 11 Outlined Epitaphs; liner notes to Times They Are A-Changin', © 1964; Liner Notes to Another Side of Bob Dylan, © 1964; I Shall Be Free #10, © 1972; Liner Notes to Bringing It All Back Home, © 1965; Liner Notes to Planet Waves, © 1973.

Contents

JIM MARSHALL

Introduction

I'm only a musician . . . .
—Bob Dylan

Bob Dylan has been acclaimed a poet, a prophet, a mystic Jewish *rebbe* and leading spiritual guru of his time. Such hyperbole aside (Dylan himself hates it most of all), he remains first and foremost a musician: a songwriter and performing artist whose genius has been to absorb and embody everything that has come before and around him into a constantly evolving synthesis of great originality and enormous influence.

This book is a history of Bob Dylan's musical development. In documenting and commenting upon the large body of work Dylan has written and produced over the years, we have inevitably chronicled much of his life in words and pictures—but our intention has been to present not a definitive biography but rather a guide to his music, particularly his recordings.

What follows, then, is a musical inventory that is truly staggering in its depth, diversity, and complexity. Dylan's influences and innovations, his changes and surprises, the layers of intention and great leaps of imagination—perhaps no American musical artist has produced more or influenced so many.

Bob Dylan has an uncanny ability to assume the mantle, to put on the masks, to adapt the styles and forms of disparate musical traditions—classical and modern, European, Appalachian, and Black—into a sophisticated musical amalgamation uniquely his own, *and* to use this music in a way that has expressed social attitudes and personal feelings, which have struck a responsive nerve in his audience and peers for a period of nearly twenty years.

By presenting this history of Bob Dylan's music, we've also tried to describe a period in American society when much of what was occurring on the cultural, political, and psychopersonal landscape was embodied and expressed through popular music and especially Bob Dylan's music. To gather and present Dylan in his totality is to celebrate great currents of thought and sensibility; to document and understand what Dylan has been expressing is to know what has happened to more than one generation since Dylan began playing and singing in the late 1950's.

Dylan is now only thirty-seven years old. There's no telling what he will do next. He's still young, healthy, ambitious, and he's never been content to rest on his laurels, so stay tuned, folks. Meanwhile, here's what he's done so far . . . .

JOSEPH SIA

***May 24, 1941.* Bob Dylan is born Robert Allen Zimmerman in Duluth, Minnesota. His father's name is Abraham; his mother's name is Beatty; five years later a younger brother, David, is born and a year after that, when Dylan is six years old, the family moves to Hibbing, Minnesota, near the Canadian border, on the great Mesabi Iron Range.**

The Zimmermans are Russian Jews, middle-class, small-business people who own a hardware, electric supply, furniture and appliance store. Dylan's family is hardworking, intelligent, supportive, not especially musical. But without any parental push or formal lessons, young Zimmerman begins playing the piano at eight or nine, then the harmonica, just picking it up himself, then—at twelve—the guitar.

Minnesota. The earth there is filled with ore; the land is very metallic and powerfully magnetic. The Indians say there's a strong spirit there, subtle and powerful and very still. Out there, against the stillness in the vast spaces of upper Minnesota—where *nobody* sings on the corners, where it's very quiet and nothing much is moving around that fast, where there's no traffic or clatter or congestion—Dylan begins to make a little noise. He starts to create a sound, and, tentatively, the sound emerges.

A shy Jewish kid among the stony-faced, strait-laced Midwesterners of Hibbing, Dylan is a loner at school, an outsider only interested in music. At thirteen he hears recordings of the great country blues singer, songwriter Hank Williams, and tries to sound like him for a while. Then he discovers "race stations," radio programs broadcast from faraway Chicago and Little Rock, Arkansas, that play black-and-blue music by Muddy Waters and Howlin' Wolf and B. B. King. Dylan listens and studies and works hard on other people's songs and styles.

In 1955, the film *Blackboard Jungle* comes to town, and like a lot of teenagers across the country, Dylan is ignited by its theme song, "Rock Around the Clock," by Bill Haley and the Comets. It's the beginning of rock 'n' roll. Dylan is knocked out by Haley and by Elvis Presley and Jerry Lee Lewis, by Buddy Holly and Chuck Berry, and particularly by Little Richard. He forms his first group, the Golden Chords, and plays around at school assemblies and talent shows. The nice, soft-spoken, chubby kid begins to dream out loud about becoming a rock 'n' roll star. At the high school's Jacket Jamboree Talent Festival, he flails and bangs away on the piano, screaming and howling like a banshee, like a teenie, white Little Richard oblivious to the ridicule of his stolid audience.

Dauntless, Dylan gets his first motorcycle, a Harley-Davidson, at fifteen and affects a James Dean style, *Rebel Without a Cause* sort of self-image, determined to make it as a musical star, listening to every record he can lay hands on, imitating and emulating the great pop and country stars of the period: Hank Snow, Bobby Vee, Bobby Freeman.

NEAL PRESTON/MIRAGE

OPPOSITE: JIM MARSHALL

"A MAJOR NEW FIGURE IN AMERICAN FOLK MUSIC"

JIM MARSHALL

MONAURAL—CL 1779
COLUMBIA
Bob
Dylan
You're No Good
Talkin' New York
In My Time of Dyin'
Man of Constant Sorrow
Fixin' to Die
Pretty Peggy-O
Highway 51
Gospel Plow
Baby, Let Me Follow You Down
House of the Risin' Sun
Freight Train Blues
Song to Woody
See That My Grave Is Kept Clean

Bob Dylan

Columbia CL 1779 and on Stereo CS 8579. Produced by John Hammond. Released February 1962. You're No Good (*Jesse Fuller*), Talkin' New York (*B. Dylan*), In My Time of Dyin', Man of Constant Sorrow (*Arranged: B. Dylan*), Fixin' to Die (*Bukka White*), Pretty Peggy-O (*Arranged: B. Dylan*); Highway 51 (*C. Jones*), Gospel Plow (*Arranged: B. Dylan*), Baby, Let Me Follow You Down (*R. Von Schmidt*), House of the Risin' Sun, Freight Train Blues, Song to Woody (*B. Dylan*), See That My Grave Is Kept Clean (*Blind Lemon Jefferson*).

DAVID GAHR

A sweet young man of twenty, cherubic and chubby-cheeked, looks out at us from the formal cover portrait of this official debut album. Beneath his cute little brown corduroy cap, Dylan's face is bathed in a dewy golden fuzz. His hands are politely folded around the neck of an acoustic guitar. He's clean and soft, and you just want to hug him to your breast or shelter him from some storm or give him chicken soup—he's such an adorable boy.

But is there something else about his eyes? Yes . . . the left one is serious, focused and intense, whereas the right one is sort of *sly,* sort of *knowing.* What else is going on beneath that look? Why is he watching us like that, hidden and veiled behind the curtained composure of that picture's pose?

We see and we hear what the album notes describe as "a major new figure in American folk music." That's the act, that's what Dylan chose to show us first time out, and there's no doubt that he's done a great job, he's brilliant at it, this "folk" album is head and shoulders above the dozens of others being released during the old-timey music craze of the early sixties. But hindsight, research, and other unreleased recordings of the same period reveal that Dylan's folksinging was only a part of the very broad musical repertory he had at that time. The unreleased *Minnesota Tapes,* recorded during precisely this period in his life, for example, show a far greater range than this first official album. The twenty-six songs he put down during that session include some hard rockers, more straight-on country music, and a broader spectrum from this student of American music than is presented in this package.

Why? Well, as Dylan said many times later, that was what was happening then in New York. He had arrived in the middle of the folk explosion and quickly rose to the top of that movement by becoming its very best musical exponent. So for now the somewhat scruffy, angel-faced boy gives us only the tip of his iceberg.

Nevertheless, this album is a virtuoso performance, with flashes and hints and seeds of Dylan's greatness—over thirty-seven minutes of fast and frenzied playing, just Mr. Dylan all by himself with his guitar and harmonica, whooping and hollering and growling and laughing; high notes, low notes, whiny and deep, fast, slow, funny, and sad. There are only two songs written by Bob himself. The rest are classics of the period, some obligatory but respectful versions of "Pretty Peggo-O" and "Man of Constant Sorrow" and "Gospel Flow," which he plays for what they're worth but which are kind of dull. And a preponderance of heavy blues songs about death like "In My Time of Dyin," "Fixin' to Die" and "See That My Grave Is Kept Clean," which were popular at the time but which seem ludicrous coming from a young man who wasn't shaving daily at the time.

Several important points emerge with the release of this first album. First of all, this fellow *can* sing. What

DAVID GAHR

phrasing! What diction! Listen to the way he pronounces *Wooooman* on the very first cut, "You're No Good." Or the way he plays with the syllables of words, emphasizing the unexpected beat of the word *Jesus* on "In My Time of Dyin'," syncopating the phrasing against the steadiness of his beat for startling emphasis. Or how he varies the tempo of his singing, rushing ahead, then slowing down again on "Baby Let Me Follow You Down." And what a vocal range. On "House of the Risin' Sun," he hits a low E, easily, then sails off to a high F. On "Freight

***June 5, 1959.* Dylan graduates from high school and moves to Minneapolis, where he enters the arts college of the University of Minnesota on a state scholarship. For a few painful months he abandons his greaser clothes for standard white bucks and sports clothes, even living for a while in a Jewish fraternity house. Soon, however, he begins to spend most of his time in Dinkytown, the bohemian Greenwich Village of Minneapolis, where he discovers that folksinging is the hippest form of musical expression around. At first he is introduced to popular versions of traditional American music through the Weavers and the Kingston Trio. Hanging out at the local coffeehouses, he quickly assumes a new persona: the beat, folksinging troubadour, scruffy and unkempt, wearing blue jeans and boots, his guitar strapped to his back, singing songs he's heard from other young singers and discovering new roots in old recordings by Jesse Fuller, Big Bill Broonzy, and other authentic folk artists. He also hears Harry Belafonte for the first time and is affected by Odetta's first album.**

The young Zimmerman lands an early gig at a coffeehouse called The Scholar, and when the owner asks his name, he thinks fast and says Bob Dylan. He also invents an imaginary past, a continually changing apocryphal personal biography, recasting his middle-class Jewish background in more romantic, outlaw fantasies, claiming to have run away from home to travel and sing with mythical folk and rock 'n' roll stars. Influenced by the radical anarchism of Dinkytown bohemia, he reads *The Grapes of Wrath* by John Steinbeck, and then — most importantly — he discovers *Bound for Glory*, the autobiography of Woody Guthrie, finding in this American folksinger the penultimate role model of his formative years.

Dylan *becomes* Guthrie. He effects a raspy, Ozark/Okie drawl, singing the great Guthrie's memorable songs — like "This Land Is Your Land," "So Long It's Been Good to Know You," "Hard Traveling," "Pastures of Plenty," "Pretty Boy Floyd," and the Dust Bowl Ballads — and also begins to write his own derivative talking-protest-folkie-blues numbers (like "Song to Woody"). He dresses like Guthrie, he talks like Guthrie, he takes on the identity of a ragged, wandering minstrel, a fascist-killer, existential hobo from the hard-time depression dust bowl — like Guthrie. Obsessed, Dylan finds in Guthrie a *raison d'etre* and musical direction for all his creative energies. He claims that he and Guthrie actually traveled around together out West and announces to friends that he must visit New Jersey, where his mentor is dying of Huntington's chorea.

Photo: With Pete Seeger

Train Blues," he holds a high C# for over thirty seconds, then skips off with a yodelly frill to a D# just a moment later. Conventional wisdom of the period has it that Dylan couldn't sing, but this first album shows that just isn't true. He is raspy and hoarse and gruff and nasal and all sorts of different things when he chooses, but each voice is assumed, it's a put-on he can change at any moment as it suits him. Underneath, his range and versatility are immense.

He can play the guitar, too. The blues work on this record is more than respectable, proving Dylan to be, in then, to play in such classy company. He has rhythm, too, for a white boy from Minnesota.

This first album, which was recorded in only three or four sessions and cost Columbia only $402, also demonstrates Dylan's eclecticism, his range of disparate styles, influences, and emulations: there's a little Everly Brothers on "Highway 51," though Dylan's rock 'n' roll roots are fairly well hidden on this album. There's plenty of Blind Lemon Jefferson and Robert Johnson on the six blues cuts. It's clear he's been listening a lot to Leadbelly and Lightnin'

what an actor Dylan has become. Each song on this record is a theatrical performance. His sense of timing and emphasis and articulation heightens the drama of every cut. Listen to the tremendous intensity, the focus of energy, the self-conscious control of power: the pause, the rush, the explosive moments of delivery. Dylan immerses himself totally and single-mindedly in each role; maybe that's why from the beginning there were always people who mistrusted him a little. Woody Guthrie and Blind Lemon Jefferson and Huddie Ledbetter and Jesse Fuller were all *real*.

JIM MARSHALL

fact, what Greil Marcus has described as "the performing curator" of American music, white *and* black. Equally exceptional is his harmonica playing. Dylan actually made his first commercial recording as a back-up harmonica player on a Big Joe Williams session produced by the legendary blues singer Victoria Spivey, whom he met performing at Gerde's Folk City in the Village. The gig was in 1961, but the record itself wasn't released until 1964 as "Three Kings and a Queen" (Williams, Roosevelt Sykes, Lonnie Johnson, and Spivey) on Spivey LP 1004. He *must* have been good, even back

Hopkins, too. Plus country-and-western stars like Jimmie Rodgers and Hank Williams. Dylan also acknowledges the material and stylistic influence he picked up from Ric Von Schmidt on "Baby, Let Me Follow You Down" but curiously fails to credit Dave Von Ronk for his version of "House of the Risin' Sun" which Dylan faithfully copies on this record. This oversight caused some strain on their friendship and provoked some grumbling in Village folk circles about Dylan's integrity versus his ruthless ambition.

But most of all this album reveals

They'd *done* what they'd sung about; they *were* men of the earth and the people and the road. Not Dylan. He knew it and we knew it. He was an actor, taking the mantle, assuming the role, playing the part. On the one hand he was brilliant; there was no one anywhere near him in talent or ability. On the other hand his calculation and ambition made people uneasy. There were always those who didn't buy the act, who considered him something inauthentic, something of a phony. Since this was clearly such a cosmic con job, they said, when would he pull out the rug, where would he go next and what was going on underneath, where was he really *at*? This doubt and resentment grew as the truth about Bob Dylan gradually emerged. In fact, much of what he said about his past experience as a wandering minstrel wasn't true. In fact, as fans discovered to their dismay, his name wasn't even Dylan; it was Zimmerman. Never mind that these were minor and unimportant details; they created from the beginning an undercurrent of suspicion and outright hostility.

Both of the original compositions on this album are classic archetypes in

DAVID GAHR

the genre of his hero and great personal influence during this period, Woody Guthrie. "Talkin' New York" is very funny and clever, sung in the nasal Guthrie voice, an excellent example of that ironic, autobiographical style. "Song to Woody," on the other hand, is sung far more simply, with reverence, veneration, and sincerity. On this famous cut, Dylan really emerges from behind the various bravura masks he's employed throughout the album to sing in a plain and gentle way to his dying hero. And he's saying So Long. Farewell. "Here's to Cisco an' Sonny an' Leadbelly, too. . . . The very last thing that I'd want to do, Is to say I've been hittin' some hard travelin', too." It's a valedictory statement not only to Woody but to a whole period of his own life. I've listened and learned, he's saying, now I'm going on to my own destiny. For in truth, Dylan realized he was no Guthrie-type hobo balladeer. He could compose and perform in that genre whenever it was appropriate. But his Guthrie-style, folksinger identity was only a phase, and this record, far from marking the debut of an important new American folkie, was really Dylan's good-bye to all that.

"*Any particular artists that you like to see do your songs?* Yeah, Elvis Presley. I liked Elvis Presley. Elvis Presley recorded a song of mine. That's the one recording I treasure the most. . . it was called "Tomorrow Is a Long Time." I wrote it but never recorded it. —Bob Dylan"

In The *Rolling Stone* Interview, © 1970 by Straight Arrow Publishers, Inc.

DAVID GAHR

Ultimately this album demonstrates Dylan's musical ability, his virtuoso playing, sophisticated singing, a broad variety of styles, within the folk and blues genres, his range of emotional performance—from comedy to tragedy—and his tremendous energy. Energy and speediness. As if Dylan himself is impatient to get on with it, to show us he can do this and then press ahead. Some of it seems hurried, rushed, clipped-off, too fast, as if he were bored. What seems most important is that Dylan *proves himself* on this album. Yes, he says, see how I can sing and play and feel all these different songs even though I'm only twenty. Watch me catch up with everything and everyone who's hot and hip in New York today. Hear how I can outholler and wail better than any of these here "folksingers" who've come before me. The secret rocker outguns the folkies at their own game. He wants to establish himself as the biggest kid on the block. **And he does!**

January 1961. **Dylan quits college and heads for New York City, where he arrives in the midst of a bitter winter's blizzard. He hitchhikes out to visit Woody Guthrie in a New Jersey institution, and the dying hero *does* like him, welcoming him on weekend trips out of hospital to a dazzling circle of musicians and performers, including Pete Seeger, Cisco Huston, Jack Elliot, Peter La Farge, Dave Von Ronk, and many others. Dylan listens and learns quickly from folk performers around the bars and coffeehouses of Greenwich Village. He works hard on the harmonica, broadens his repertoire, and begins to get gigs at a few spots like the Cafe Wha?, the Gaslight, and particularly at Gerde's Folk City where he opens as a warm-up act for the Greenbriar Boys. Robert Shelton of *The New York Times* sees him there and is inspired to write on September 29, 1961, an exceptionally favorable review about this charismatic young man, "resembling a cross between a choir boy and a beatnik. . . bursting at the seams with talent." Dylan now wears a Huck Finn black corduroy cap and affects Chaplinesque comedy routines between his songs. He's adorable; he's unique and original; he's rising very rapidly among the ranks of folksingers, quickly assimilating and surpassing all the skills and materials around him.**

Still very much the Guthrie-style folkie, however, Dylan writes "Talking Bear" and "Talkin' New York" in the then-popular thirties mode. He wangles a job playing back-up harmonica at a Carolyn Hester recording session for Columbia Records. One day at the studio, the distinguished record producer John Hammond—who's previously recorded Bessie Smith, Billy Holliday, and other giants—hears Dylan is enthralled, and offers him an unprecedented recording contract. With this stroke of good fortune, Dylan cuts his first solo album at the age of twenty.

THE FREEWHEELIN' BOB DYLAN

Blowin' in the Wind
Girl From the North Country
Masters of War
Down the Highway
Bob Dylan's Blues
A Hard Rain's A-Gonna Fall

Don't Think Twice, It's All Right
Bob Dylan's Dream
Oxford Town
Talkin' World War III Blues
Corrina, Corrina
Honey, Just Allow Me One More Chance
I Shall Be Free

The Freewheelin' Bob Dylan

Columbia CL 1968 and on Stereo CS 8786. Produced by John Hammond. Released May 1963. Blowin' in the Wind (*B. Dylan*), Girl from the North Country (*B. Dylan*), Masters of War (*B. Dylan*), Down the Highway (*B. Dylan*), Bob Dylan's Blues (*B. Dylan*), A Hard Rain's A-Gonna Fall (*B. Dylan*); Don't Think Twice, It's All Right (*B. Dylan*), Bob Dylan's Dream (*B. Dylan*), Oxford Town (*B. Dylan*), Talking World War III Blues (*B. Dylan*), Corrina, Corrina (*Adapted and arranged: B. Dylan*), Honey, Just Allow Me One More Chance (*H. Thomas and B. Dylan*), I Shall Be Free (*B. Dylan*).

Bob Dylan's second album had an extraordinary impact upon its first release, and it remains an historic event today. It showed us much more of what he could do. Only twenty-one years old but, my, how he was learning and growing and pushing further ahead, exploring and taking chances and breaking new ground for all of us to follow.

After the more deferential, less personal politesse of his first album, this *Freewheelin'* Bob Dylan throws open all the windows and tears the sheets off the furniture. This is not the work of a pious folksinger, nossir, this young fellow has written twelve out of thirteen songs on this album himself and practically no two are the same: there are passionate love songs and crashing apocalyptic visions; there's talking blues and singing blues, a long bombastic protest song, a short ironic protest song, a titillating glimpse of rock 'n' roll, some nasty comic stuff, and to top it all off, an immortal spiritual anthem which made him famous everywhere and opens up this album: "Blowin in the Wind."

"Blowin' in the Wind" has withstood the test of time. It stands as a song not just for a special period or generation but for all time and every generation. It's universal—the melody, the words, the experience of singing it either alone or in a group make it work in China, Russia, Europe, Africa, Latin America, and the U.S. of A. The effect is so spiritually cathartic, it's like chanting from Ecclesiastes. It's biblical. Specifically it's Old Testament and traditionally Jewish, particularly with Dylan's device of answering questions with yet more questions. And the answer? Is it blowing *away*? Won't we ever *know*? Or is it just blowing *by*, just waiting to be realized? Is it like the *ein sof*, the Judaic unknowable divine deity beyond all human comprehension? Or is it like the Zen fountain, the cosmic giggle, the onion of life so easy to see, how could we overlook it?

Dylan doesn't say. Rather he leaves us with some eternal observations: that everything is one; that we're all separate but we're all the same; that therefore each of us is responsible to the other. When will we break through our existential isolation to universal love? And how can we reconcile this divine connection with the universal godhead with our puny, mortal feelings of isolation, loneliness, and

February 1962. **Dylan's first album sells only 5,000 copies upon its initial release. His ability and reputation as a songwriter, however, continue to grow as he produces a series of extraordinary contemporary compositions with stunning lyrics and powerful musical force in an impassioned response to the cataclysmic political events in the air around him. For concurrent with his emergence on the New York scene is the early sixties explosion of social protest against racism and the very real threat of nuclear warfare.**

JIM MARSHALL

Bob's political consciousness, as well as his creativity and growth as a loving man, are influenced during this period by his friend Suze Rotolo. Their romance inspires several important songs, and Suze herself appears with her lover, arm in arm, walking down a Village street on the cover photograph for this second album.

Photo: With Pete Seeger at Newport Folk Festival, 1963

Acutely sensitive and quick to respond, Dylan writes "Blowin' in the Wind" in April. Then "Masters of War," "Hard Rain," "Oxford Town," and other enormously popular "protest" songs, which are inspired by the news of the day and the continuing storm of emotional political events raging through this period, e.g. civil-rights protests and murders, the Cuban missile crisis.

death? Don't ask me, he says. But the act of asking itself helps us take a little step toward each other, feel a bit more responsible, love a little more. Dylan sings it straight from the heart, too, quite simply, directly, without artifice. It's the first of a succession of moralistic religious sermons written by Dylan, the teacher, the *rabbi.*

"Girl from the North Country" is a beautiful, passionate reminiscence of lost love, far away and long ago. It's about Echo Star Helstrom, Bob Dylan's high-school sweetheart, a lovely blonde Swedish girl from his hometown, Hibbing, Minnesota, who was an important friend and influence during those early outlaw years. Singing with conviction, honesty, and tenderness, Dylan's voice ranges from an emotional high lyricism to an intimate lower resonance; his breathing is careful and deliberate, his elucidation of the words wonderful in its precision. The obvious respect, the evocation of sexuality and gentle humor—no wonder this song, too, has remained so popular through the years since. It demonstrates a surprising maturity and sophistication about love, particularly when compared to some of the other "love" songs Dylan was writing during this period, which are full of bitterness and spite.

"Masters of War" has been acclaimed as a landmark "protest" song, then and now. Dylan once sang it for me in a little studio at the offices of the Whitmark Publishing Company, and I was so bored I couldn't stop squirming. It was so simplistic, so two-dimensionally absolute, so long and tiresome. How can you be so subtle and complex with "Blowin' in the Wind," I said, then so bombastic and adolescent about so-called "Masters." Who are these straw men, these stereotypes? They simply don't exist. I agree with your politics, but this kind of overkill is just plain silly . . . . Bob ignored me and sang on, his teeth bared in venom and vituperation. And he was right. The song became famous. People loved it. History vindicated his judgment, his keen sense of what millions of young people were experiencing.

"Masters of War" struck a nerve. It, too, became a popular anthem, reflecting the tenor of its time, the early sixties, the civil-rights movement, the peace movement, the rise of white student rebellion. Though as I stood by the stage while Dylan performed this song at the March on Washington in August of 1963, I heard a few black people asking each other "Who is this, what's he saying, when's the song over . . . ." and saw them drifting away.

"A Hard Rain's A-Gonna Fall," on the other hand, is a different kind of protest song: artfully contrived, carefully delivered, one of the most substantial creative accomplishments of this album. Opening with a Lord Randal-style question, "Oh, where have you been, my blue-eyed son?" Dylan proceeds to catalog the horrors of nuclear holocaust, painting a brilliant apocalyptic vision of nightmarish hell, crystallizing the sense of terror and impending doom that many people felt during the Cuban missile crisis of October 1962, when this song was written. "It's a desperate kind of song," Dylan said at the time. "When I wrote it, I thought I wouldn't have enough time alive to write all those songs, so I put all I could into this one . . . every line in it is actually the start of a whole song."

The compressed images are at the same time devastatingly awful and hauntingly lovely:

I met a young child beside a dead pony,
I met a white man who walked a black dog,
I met a young woman whose body was burning,
I met a young girl, she gave me a rainbow,
I met one man who was wounded in love,
I met another man who was wounded with hatred.

What a catalog! What declamation! What effective rhetoric! First he wails like a crazed Jewish cantor through

DAVID GAHR

JIM MARSHALL

Above: With Suze Rotolo
Right: With Suze Rotolo and Dave Von Ronk in Greenwich Village

JIM MARSHALL

"My mind was with the music . . . that feeling that was in the air. I tried to somehow get a hold of that, and write that down, and using my musical training to sort of guide it by, and in the end, have something I could do for a living.

I can remember traveling through towns, and if somebody played the guitar, that's who you went to see . . . to watch them, listen to them and if possible, learn how to do something . . . whatever he was doing . . . . It wasn't necessarily a song; it was technique and style, and tricks and all those combinations which go together—which I certainly spent a lot of hours just trying to do what other people have been doing. That's what I mean by training. —Bob Dylan"

From *Conversations with Bob Dylan* by John Cohen & Happy Traum, *Sing Out!*, October-November, 1968

JIM MARSHALL

JIM MARSHALL

this litany of beauty and horrors. Then he pounds ominously into the hard, hard refrain, the rain of nuclear catastrophe to come. And in our secret hearts the song reminds us that, if it isn't nuclear fallout, it will be something else. The song is really an effective metaphor for *all* dread of death and violence, for the dark side: the underbelly of love and beauty, the loss of youth and life from whence there's no escape, friends, because none of us is going to get out of this alive.

"Don't Think Twice, It's All Right" is a charming, nasty number, the first of a succession of songs Dylan's written that say so long to a woman. In this case, it's probably Suze Rotolo he's so upset about. She'd grown weary of Dylan's newfound notoriety and rapidly changing persona and, in defiance, sailed off with her mother and her sister to Italy, where she remained out of contact with Dylan for several months. Sung in a wry, humorous style, accompanied by guitar and harmonica, the gentle arrangement belies the cutting edge of the lyrics:

I once loved a woman, a child I'm told
I give her my heart but she wanted my soul. . . .
You could have done better but I don't mind
You just kinda wasted my precious time. . . .

And the ironic refrain: "Don't think twice, it's all right. . . ." As if to say, "You silly thing, go ahead and forget it, I'll just limp along inflicted with your pain." A little one-sided, you say? A little self-pitying? But what a great put-down, yes? After all, as Dylan himself says on the album's liner notes, "It's a statement that maybe you can say to make yourself feel better." An interesting self-revelation, since in fact there is a continuing delicate balance in this number between bitterness and a kind of happy-go-lucky, whistle-in-the-dark optimism. And it's precisely the tension of this tight-wire act that gives the song its power. Darkness and light; self-pity versus self-irony; the words versus the music.

This kind of duality also appears in "Oxford Town," a cute ditty, whose musical flippancy contrasts sharply with the "guns and clubs" of Oxford, Mississippi, where two men died when a black man, James Meredith, tried to enter the university. "Talking World War III Blues" is a comic version of "Hard Rain." This time Dylan dreams he's one of the few survivors of the ultimate nuclear holocaust. As he comes out from the sewer, people start shooting at him from fallout shelters (remember them?). When he asks a girl to play Adam and Eve, she says, "Hey, man, you crazy or sumpin'? You see what happened last time they

Columbia Records is confused and somewhat lukewarm about Dylan's future, but through the insistence of John Hammond and with the support of Johnny Cash, they agree to produce a second album which will demonstrate Dylan's rapid growth as an artist who performs his own music. Meanwhile, Dylan is invited to appear on the *Ed Sullivan Show,* but the TV censors won't let him sing "The Talkin' John Birch Society Blues," so he walks away, refusing to appear. Moreover, Columbia Records censors this same song from Dylan's second album. He's incensed and fights for its reinstatement, but at this point he hasn't got the success or the clout to overcome their veto.

DAVID GAHR

started." It's all very light and funny in this version, but just as awful. Lucky it's only a dream, but as he says ominously at the end of the song, "I'll let you be in my dreams if I can be in yours," followed by the cocky coda: "*I* said that." He wants to be in our dreams, does he? He may deny it elsewhere, but it's true. Like an inner voice, a consciousness or a *conscience,* he wants us to listen.

There's an erroneous reference in the liner notes to a back-up band on "Don't Think Twice." The version released on this album has Dylan alone. This band, however, does appear on "Corrina, Corrina," an old song which Dylan has adapted. Bruce Langhorne (guitar), George Barnes (bass guitar), Dick Wellstood (piano), Gene Ramey (bass), and Herb Lovelle (drums) play rather quietly behind Dylan's vocal, which is quite different from anything else on the album.

In the early sixties, most people thought Dylan couldn't sing. Robert Shelton himself, whose review of young Dylan in *The New York Times* was instrumental in bringing Dylan to the public eye wrote "Dylan's voice is anything but pretty . . . ." and goes on to describe its "rude beauty . . . [and] . . . husk and bark." In those days, Dylan's delivery *was* exceptional, folks hadn't heard anything like it. But I think he was good even then, and he's been getting better since, developing new voices and styles, picking up new vocal techniques and improving all along.

On "Corrina, Corrina" Dylan shows us a little bit of the old rocker from high-school days. There's a touch of Buddy Holly on the refrain "Baby, please come home . . . ." and that little vibrato in the falsetto, it's not unlike, could it be, Elvis Presley? Funny nobody noticed this at the time, and with all the electric backing, too. Fact is, this cut is pretty nearly real rock 'n' roll. Not only that, during the same *Freewheelin'* session Dylan made a real rocker called "Mixed-up Confusion" with this same back-up band. Columbia released this song as a single, then withdrew it quickly when it didn't sell. They concluded that the market wasn't ready for Dylan to come out of his rock closet yet. They may have been right, judging from the furor created two years later when Dylan finally did go public with his true electric identity. But had everyone paid closer attention to "Corrina" and "Mixed-up Confusion," the transition might have been somewhat less painful for all concerned.

"Honey, Just Allow Me One More Chance" credits a co-writer named Henry Thomas, from whom Dylan claims to have heard this number first. The singing is a riot: whooping and shouting like Jerry Lee Lewis—speeding through the verses, but with every word clearly understood. Very funny, very droll, very witty.

Honey, just allow me one more chance
To ride your aeroplane.
Honey, just allow me one more chance
To ride your passenger train.

A little double-entendre, laced with some heavier lines like "I'm lookin' for a woman needs a worried man . . . ." Tongue-in-cheek, down on his knees, kidding but dead serious, too, it's one of the best performances on this record.

Dylan arranges the order of the songs on his albums with utmost care. It's no accident, therefore, that he concludes this *Freewheelin'* record with "I Shall Be Free," a self-celebratory, very high, autobiographical festivity. It's Dylan with his clothes off, drunk and sexy, funny and disrespectful and full of himself, he even has

JIM MARSHALL

JIM MARSHALL

JIM MARSHALL

July 1963. **Dylan's second album is a far greater success than his first, selling over 200,000 copies within a short period of its release. Peter, Paul, and Mary record two songs from this record, "Blowin' in the Wind" and "Don't Think Twice," and these singles become monster hits on the AM Top Forty charts. Dylan himself is wildly cheered at the Newport Folk Festival, hailed by audience and peers alike as "the most important folk artist in America today." Joan Baez begins to sing many of his songs and brings him onstage for the second half of her performances. The "Queen" introduces her Crown Prince to a far larger, adoring new audience, which begins to accept him as their spokesman.**

DAVID GAHR

President Kennedy calling up to ask him for advice:

He said, "My friend, Bob, what do we
need to make the country grow?"
I said, "My friend, John, Brigitte
Bardot,
Anita Ekberg,
Sophia Loren."

If Dylan is feeling his oats in this funny, irreverent song, it's a fitting climax to a virtuoso production. For anyone who had any doubts, this second album proved that Bob Dylan was a very major talent and an enormous influence both on his public and on other artists. More and more people knew about Dylan and were affected by the originality of his work. He had made all sorts of new possibilities available to other writers and performing artists; he had opened many doors to a variety of styles and personal expressions that had never before been thought possible in the arena of pop music.

The range of *Freewheelin'* is tremendous: humor, anger, bombast, wit; loveliness, loneliness, irony, and spit (it's catching!). His ability to reflect not only his own feelings but some simpler, more general emotions he felt around him, was uncanny. And however mythic, two-dimensional, or adolescent these feelings were, he was usually able to rescue them with the brilliance of his music and his performance.

No longer just another Guthrie imitator, Dylan hammers out his own eclectic style of playing and singing. The music still derives from black and country and folk traditions, but the ***words*** **and the** ***voice*** **strike a new nerve. No one has ever written pop songs like this before: his lyrics are poetic and deeply personal—shades of Rimbaud, William Blake, Baudelaire, James Joyce, and Allen Ginsberg appear in his work—and he uses both real incidents and symbolic metaphors to express the passion and the violence of his own life and times.**

OVERLEAF: JIM MARSHALL

LAUNDRY
NO PARKING
FLORENCE
LAUNDRY
WE TURN COLLARS
GARAGE
DAY PARKING
SA

PROTEST AND APOCALYPSE

JIM MARSHALL

MONO—CL 2105

THE TIMES THEY ARE A-CHANGIN'

BOB DYLAN

THE LONESOME DEATH OF HATTIE CARROLL
BOOTS OF SPANISH LEATHER
RESTLESS FAREWELL / WITH GOD ON OUR SIDE
THE TIMES THEY ARE A-CHANGIN'
ONLY A PAWN IN THEIR GAME

WHEN THE SHIP COMES IN / ONE TOO MANY MORNINGS
BALLAD OF HOLLIS BROWN / NORTH COUNTRY BLUES

The Times They Are A-Changin'

Columbia Mono CL 2105 or Stereo KCS 8905. Produced by Tom Wilson. Released January 1964. The Times They Are A-Changin', Ballad of Hollis Brown, With God on Our Side, One Too Many Mornings, North Country Blues; Only a Pawn in Their Game, Boots of Spanish Leather, When the Ship Comes In, The Lonesome Death of Hattie Carroll, Restless Farewell. *All written by Bob Dylan.*

As an astute salesman for himself and his music, Bob Dylan began to understand the importance of album packaging. Consequently, as his success and significance at Columbia Records grew, he tried to exercise more control over what appeared on the front and back of his albums. The first album introduced a carefully posed still life: the portrait of the artist as a young folksinger. The second album showed us a carefree young man bounding down the streets of Greenwich Village with his lovely lady, Suze Rotolo. Both were in full color. This third album, *The Times They Are A-Changin'* presents a radically and deliberately different image: a hard-eyed, tough-looking hombre in a coarse work shirt against a two-color, black-on-tan background. This is a new image and a new identity: Bob Dylan, Protest Singer.

This album was recorded in September and October of 1963, the peak year of the civil-rights movement. Demonstrations and bombings and murders racked the South. In August, the March on Washington had galvanized revolutionary political consciousness—particularly among the young—throughout the country. John F. Kennedy was President and there was a feeling of hope and impending change. And riding on top of it all, capturing its essential feeling and firing it on with anthems and exhortations was Bob Dylan, known in his first public, mass-market incarnation as primarily a singer of "protest songs."

And for good reason. Most of the songs on this album are devastating in their power of political persuasion. The title song is a solemn, dead-serious sermon delivered in a flat, righteous voice with a heavy drone-like beat. And that name, the repeated litany of that declaration: *The Times They Are A-Changin'.* It sounds like an expression we've known all our lives or heard a lot somewhere, before. But we haven't. Dylan just made it up, the perfect expression of our sentiment, our innate desire. If ever a song crystallized the passions of a generation, it's this one. Out of the mouths of babes . . . a young man warns his elders, the message is loud and clear: shape up, fly right, make way or else. You writers and critics, you Senators and Congressmen—we'll shake your windows, you'll sink like a stone—it's threatening, it's as frightening as a prophetic incantation from the Old Testament. Isaiah, Jeremiah, and now Dylan (*nēe* Zimmer-

In so doing, Dylan takes popular music to a higher level, elevating it far above the shallow restrictions of Tin Pan Alley and creating a powerful new vehicle for social, political, and personal expression. Hearing Dylan for the first time, young artists like John Lennon are stunned and excited; they feel released from past prohibitions and inspired to express their own revolutionary feelings and ideas within the traditional forms that Dylan has liberated. Literally hundreds of other artists and performers follow his lead, and pop is never the same again.

DAVID GAHR

Fame, however, muddles and complicates Dylan's life, bringing with it tremendous stresses and increasing public pressure. Old friends drop away or are discarded. His relationship with Suze Rotolo suffers greatly, and their estrangement grows. And the role of Albert Grossman, Dylan's new manager and father protector, looms ominously larger. Grossman tries unsuccessfully to renegotiate Dylan's contract with Columbia Records. Grossman complains that Columbia doesn't understand Dylan. Under this hostile pressure John Hammond steps aside, suggesting that Dylan's third album be produced by a young A&R man, Tom Wilson.

October 1963. Bob Dylan's debut concert at Carnegie Hall sells out to an adoring crowd of screaming fans, including his proud parents, Abraham and Beatty, flown in for the best seats in the house. _Newsweek_ magazine, piqued by Dylan's evasiveness and Grossman's paranoia, takes this opportunity to lambast Zimmerman as a phony poseur who has changed his name and denied his bourgeois, middle-class background (palpably true) and perhaps also stolen his best song "Blowin' in the Wind" (completely false). This further aggravates his alienation from the media but also underlines his own ambivalent self-image.

November 1963. President John F. Kennedy is assassinated. Dylan, like everyone else, is stunned. Dylan, like everyone else, feels a cynical shift in attitude toward politics and the hope for positive social change. Appearing before the Emergency Civil Liberties Committee to accept their prestigious Tom Paine Award, he drinks too much, offends his audience of affluent liberals, and is increasingly estranged from formal political organizations and activities.

man) chant acocalyptic portents of doom. There may be some hope for a few young survivors, but it looks pretty grim for most of you parents and teachers and grown-ups.

This first cut is an angry, strident song and bitter, too, for such a young man to have written. But it works because the drama of Dylan's poetry and music and intense performance are able to elevate that adolescent righteousness to a truly high moral level. We believe. He's *right.* Parts of this sound as though they were carved in stone by divine power or found on some tablets in a sacred holy cave on Mount Sinai:

The line it is drawn
The curse it is cast
The slow one now
Will later be fast
As the present now
Will later be past
The order is
Rapidly fadin'.
And the first one now
Will later be last
For the times they are a-changin'.

Powerful stuff. It fires the blood. Thousands raised their voices, hundreds of thousands joined together, marching down the streets with this and other songs by Dylan in their hearts and minds.

The second song on this album is "The Ballad of Hollis Brown," the true story of a poor South Dakota farmer who slaughters his wife and five children and then himself, in an act of desperate hopeless misery. Dylan tells the tragic story in a traditional, eleven-verse ballad form. Although the boring, bombastic, repetitious quality doesn't hold up well with time, this song was nevertheless quite popular upon its release.

The following cut continues the relentless harangue of this "protesting" album. "With God on Our Side" is a brilliant, quick lesson in the hypocrisy and savagery of American history, an ironic survey of patriotic killings from the cowboys versus the Indians to the Cold War. Dylan assumes the persona of a Brechtian Everyman bewildered and confused by the contradiction of political wars waged in the name of morality. First we kill the Germans, now they're our friends. Now we hate the Russians.

I'm weary as Hell
The confusion I'm feelin'.

Dylan's performance is highly theatrical, employing a recitative style of spoken delivery, with pauses and rushes and biting, emphatic phrasing. He's an actor, but this part comes from the heart:

Ain't no tongue can tell
The words fill my head
And fall to the floor
If God's on our side
He'll stop the next war.

Remember: back then people felt that doomsday was a very real possibility . . . maybe just around the corner.

What's most interesting about the song "One Too Many Mornings" is that it is nearly identical in melody and

DAVID GAHR

FRED W. McDARRAH

Photo: With Joan Baez and Paul Stookey (of Peter, Paul and Mary) at The Lincoln Memorial during the March on Washington, 1963

FRED W. McDARRAH

JIM MARSHALL

March 1964. **After months of anguished comings and goings, Bob and Suze Rotolo finally break up. It takes him a long time to get over it. Many songs are written about this rupture. . . . Meanwhile Dylan's relationship with Joan Baez is rumored to have become more than professional.**

Photo: Onstage with Peter, Paul and Mary, The Student Non-Violent Coordinating Committee's Freedom Singers, Pete Seeger and Theodore Bikel

May 1964. Dylan performs a concert tour of England, where he meets the Rolling Stones and Eric Burdon of the Animals. In London, he turns the Beatles on to marijuana, making friends with Paul McCartney and John Lennon. The Beatles and their music thrill him. They influence him as much as he has influenced them, and he returns to America determined to assert himself in new directions. He feels more secure as an artist, ready to write strictly for himself; and he envies the possibilities of playing among other musicians in a band, with all the musical variations possible therein.

© 1967 DANIEL KRAMER

OPPOSITE: JIM MARSHALL

Opposite: Newport 1964

> "Dylan created a myth that already existed. In a very real sense we could call it the myth of our own purity. Dylan was the only one on the scene who had the self-awareness, charisma, talent, imagination and lack of repression to give structure to this world view."
> —Jon Landau
>
> Crawdaddy! 1968

harmonic progression to "The Times They Are A-Changin'." It's interesting to see how Dylan has taken many of the same musical ingredients to say something completely different and far more personal in this sad song of two lovers' separation, as if to say see how I can separate my real self from the rhetoric of my public protest songs *within the same musical structure.* There's only a glimmer of this dichotomy, this difference between the public stance and the private person, on this album. But as we shall see, it doesn't stay under wraps for long.

In "North Country Blues," Dylan speaks as a woman, and a miserable story she, too, has to tell. Poverty, misery, abandonment. It's a relief to move on to the next cut, "Only a Pawn in Their Game," which is a very witty, wise, and compassionate song about the murder of Medgar Evers. In contrast to the black and white simplism of some of his other songs, Dylan here sees the villain as victim. The killer can't really be blamed, he's only "the caboose of the train," poor and dumb and dehumanized. Listen to this:

And he's taught how to walk in a pack
Shoot in the back
With his fist in a clinch
To hang and to lynch
To hide 'neath the hood
To kill with no pain
Like a dog on a chain
He ain't got no name
But it ain't him to blame
He's only a pawn in their game.

A devastating analysis of southern society, far more effective, I think, than the pious absolutism of "Masters of War." The politicians are still making the real moves in this metaphor, but there's a funny sort of tenderness and pity for the poor white-trash killer who's only an anonymous fool beside the "king" that he's slain.

"Boots of Spanish Leather" is another startling change of pace from the preponderance of heavy, protest songs on this album. This warm, lyrical romantic love song has a wonderfully haunting progression of chord changes, from F#m9 to E7(D7) and tells a charming, sad story: his lover is leaving, and he doesn't know when (or even if) she'll return. What can she send him from far across the sea? Not silver or gold or diamonds, better a kiss or a letter . . . but after nine verses of painful loss and tenderness, he says, oh, yes, can you send me some boots of Spanish leather? Quite simple. Very touching. Dylan has let us see something very intimate and personal; his vulnerability, his gentle parts. And whereas all the other strident protestations go on, mark this

REX FEATURES

well because it's an important thread; it reveals a large soft part of him at the center, which is far more important than any of the suits of armor he puts on to do battle with the puppet masters.

Lest we relax, however, this lovely number is followed by the ominous and scary "When the Ship Comes In," a ballad strongly reminiscent of the famous "Pirate Jenny" song by Kurt Weill and Bertolt Brecht from *The Threepenny Opera.* As in that bitter anthem so brilliantly performed by Lotte Lenya, the forces of evil, the singer's foes, are jerked from their beds and destroyed by the arrival of a great menacing ship, a mysterious, supernatural force that arrives, breaking the chains of the sea, to wreak vengeance upon the unrighteous without pity or remorse:

Then they'll raise their hands,
Sayin' we'll meet all your demands,
But we'll shout from the bow your days
are numbered.
And like Pharoah's tribe,
They'll be drowned in the tide,
And like Goliath, they'll be
conquered.

© 1967 DANIEL KRAMER

July 1964.* Dylan surprises his audience at the annual Newport Folk Festival by deliberately singing personal compositions about love, rather than his usual protest songs. This calculated transition is escalated with the appearance of his new, more clearly autobiographical fourth album, *Another Side of Bob Dylan.

"I only look at them [the lyrics] musically, I only look at them as things to sing. It's the music that the words are sung to that's important. I write the songs because I need something to sing. —Bob Dylan"

In Dylan is Back by Hubert Saal © Newsweek, Inc. 1968

You could call this a somewhat uncompromising view of social revolution. Taken with the other songs on this album, it presents a violent and frightening view of revolutionary change. Does Dylan mean it? You bet he does! He's expressing both the general gut feelings of that time and his own strong sense of personal morality. He *does* feel tremendous rage and compassion and anger and sorrow, particularly in the song he later says moved him most on this album: "The Lonesome Death of Hattie Carroll." This is the story of a fifty-one year-old black mother of ten, a maid murdered by a rich boy whom the court lets off with a six-month sentence. More than in "Hollis Brown," Dylan here touches our hearts, asking us to hold off on our feelings until we hear the whole story, deliberately manipulating our emotions for the first three verses of the song:

But you who philosophize disgrace
and criticize all fears
Take the rag away from your face.
Now ain't the time for your tears. . . .

Until the devastatingly unjust verdict comes on the fourth verse, when he asks us to experience the full force of this miscarriage, releasing us to

Bury the rag deep in your face
For now's the time for your tears.

"Restless Farewell," the valedictory song of this album, seems to say goodbye not only to his audience, but in a deeper sense to that part of himself which this cycle of songs has represented. After slaying all those dragons and tilting at windmills throughout these strident protest songs, Dylan stoically laments:

Oh ev'ry foe that ever I faced,
The cause was there before we came.
And ev'ry cause that ever I fought,
I fought it full without regret or shame.
But the dark does die
As the curtain is drawn and
somebody's eyes
Must meet the dawn.

He seems to be saying, okay, folks, that was my reaction to the world I found these past few years, those were the thoughts "strung in a knot in my mind" that had to be "sprung." But I'm moving on. Start the revolution without me, I'm *not* going to lead you into battle, I'm an artist, a private person. He withdraws. He refuses to be our creature, our fantasy, our heroic model. . . .

And the dirt of gossip blows into my
face,
And the dust of rumors covers me . . .
So I'll make my stand
And remain as I am
And bid farewell and not give a damn.

Dylan's shown us his vision. He's given us ample rhetoric and political anthems for our cause. But he won't play any parts; he's no Jerry Rubin or Rap Brown. He bridles at classification. Whatever you think I am, he says, I'm not.

Times They Are A-Changin' marks the first time Dylan himself has written the liner notes for one of his albums. In "11 Outlined Epitaphs" he struggles through twelve single-spaced columns of verse to express his true self:

Yes I am a thief of thoughts
not, I pray, a stealer of souls . . .
no I must react and spit fast
with weapons of words
wrapped in tunes . . .
they can build me up
according t their own terms
so that they are able
t bust me down

So let none of us assume that the grim-visaged, broadside singer on the album photo of this latest release is the definitive Bob Dylan. Not by a long shot. That's *not* all, folks. It's just a piece of my puzzle, and there's much more to come.

REX FEATURES

TRUCE

JIM MARSHALL

Another side of Bob Dylan

All I Really Want To Do
Black Crow Blues
Spanish Harlem Incident
Chimes Of Freedom
I Shall Be Free No. 10
To Ramona
Motorpsycho Nitemare
My Back Pages
I Don't Believe You
Ballad In Plain D
It Ain't Me Babe

Another Side of Bob Dylan

Columbia Stereo KCS 8993 or Mono CL 2193. Produced by Tom Wilson. Released August 1964. All I Really Want to Do, Black Crow Blues, Spanish Harlem Incident, Chimes of Freedom, I Shall Be Free No. 10, To Ramona; Motorpsycho Nitemare, My Back Pages, I Don't Believe You, Ballad in Plain D, It Ain't Me Babe. *All written by Bob Dylan.*

The cover of Bob Dylan's fourth official album is the most subdued to date. Lots of white space. A smaller, more enigmatic photograph of the artist. And that deliberate title: *Another* side. *Not* the folksinger. *Not* the writer of protest songs. This album is a conscious effort to get away from that, to break free of any constricting stereotypes, get off the soapbox and turn inward. Consequently this album has an emphasis on love rather than rhetoric, on relationships rather than revolution. A full eight of the eleven songs are about women. Nevertheless there's still an undertone of anger and apocalypse to many of the songs and not only in those which are still overtly political, as we shall see.

"All I Really Want to Do," for example, poses as a plea for peace with a woman. "Truce!" he sings in so many words:

I ain't lookin' to compete with you,
Beat or cheat or mistreat you,
Simplify you, classify you,
Deny, defy or crucify you.
All I really want to do
Is, baby, be friends with you.

This brilliant internal rhyming system is the sort John Lennon began to use in the early 1970's. And the singing is wonderful: Dylan hits a high B-flat that's not to be believed. But there's also an edge in his voice that contradicts this apparent offer of conciliatory mutual respect. Little explosions of demonic laughter break through from time to time, particularly toward the end of the song. Some women listening to this performance might become quite wary: Is he telling the truth? Or is he a wolf in sheep's clothing? Listen to how *well* he describes all these terrible things to inflict upon a woman: frighten, tighten, drag, drain, chain, shock, knock, lock, analyze, categorize, race, chase, disgrace, displace, define, confine, dissect, inspect, reject, shake, forsake . . . this fellow is an expert. Perhaps he doth protest *too much.* Watch out! With a friend like this, you may not need any enemies. Again, Dylan the Gemini, the dual personality, the two in one, is telling us opposite things at the same time. It's paradoxical.

Dylan is clearly trying to mix them up on this album, presenting a far greater variety of musical styles than on *The Times They Are A'Changin'.* There were *no* blues numbers on that third album, for example, whereas the next cut "Black Crow Blues" provides some positively wicked piano playing.

JIM MARSHALL

JIM MARSHALL

> Many people hate Bob Dylan because they hate being fooled. . . . —Ellen Willis

In *Cheetah,* © 1967 by Ellen Willis

Sounds like a "treated" instrument, doctored somehow (perhaps with thumbtacks stuck in the hammers) to get that rickety-tin, slightly off-key effect. In any case, Dylan delivers this flat-out black-and-blue number with funky verve on the keyboard and on his harp. "Spanish Harlem Incident" is another song for a woman, the first of a series of love songs with a Latin theme, this one written for a gypsy, a flaming New York Puerto Rican lady with pearly eyes and diamond teeth. It's also one of a succession of songs wherein Dylan claims that his reality, his very existence, is aided and abetted, even positively defined, by the love of a woman:

JIM MARSHALL

32

I got to know, babe, will I be
touching you
So I can tell if I'm really real.

This is no exaggeration. Here and elsewhere, Dylan repeats this theme: his existence, his identity, the security of his being, is defined by his relationship with a woman, by his love.

"Chimes of Freedom" would appear to be a leftover political protest song, but these bells are ringing for no particular parochial cause, but for "every hung-up person in the whole wide universe . . . for each an' ev'ry underdog . . . ," a somewhat broader inclusion than previously recorded. All-inclusive, pansympathetic, overstated in its repetition, tedious in its exhausting listless catalog of "refugees, the rebel, the luckless, the outcast, the gentle, the mistreated, countless confused, accused, misused, strung-out ones an' worse." But this song was one of Dylan's most popular at the time. It seemed to capture the last gasp of hope for the underdog after the devastating blow of John Kennedy's death.

"I Shall Be Free #10," reminiscent of the last cut on the *Freewheelin'* album, is one of the most enjoyable and delightful songs on this album. In one of his flattest, drollest style voices, Dylan does his just plain Uncle Bob act:

I'm just average, common too
I'm just like him, the same as you . . . .

We don't believe it, but it sure is funny. He doesn't believe it, either.

Yippii! I'm a poet, and I know it.
Hope I don't blow it.

He's having a good time, playing with us, playing with himself, repeating a musical fillip—a catchy, clever little musical phrase—teasing us with it as he teases us with the meaning of the song itself, then saying it's nothing, just nothing . . . .

Now you're probably wondering by
now
Just what this song is all about
What's probably got you baffled more
Is what this thing [*the musical phrase*]
is for.
It's nothing
It's something I learned over in
England.

First he tricks us into liking, even loving something, loving him in fact. Then he tells us it's nothing and by the way this ain't me either . . . . "Many people," as Ellen Willis writes, "hate Bob Dylan because they hate being fooled."

"To Ramona" could have been a

> "Getting married, having a bunch of kids, I have no hopes for it. If it happens, it happens. . . . I don't think things can turn out, that's all, and I've accepted it. It doesn't matter to me. It's not pessimism, just a sort of sadness. . . . I've been connected so many times. Things haven't worked out right, so rather than break myself up, I just don't get connected. —Bob Dylan"

Interview with Joseph Haas. *Chicago Daily News,* 1965

country-and-western hit if it had been arranged differently. And maybe someday it will. Here Dylan does, however, show that other side: the tender, more vulnerable boy who wrote "Girl from the North Country" and "Boots of Spanish Leather." . . . "Motorpsycho Nitemare" is a funny talking song, a long take-off on the old "traveling salesman" stories, with Dylan in the role of a bratty adolescent taunting the poor farmer with his love of Fidel Castro.

"My Back Pages" is the most serious and revealing song on this album, a fascinating and important piece of self-analysis. For whereas Dylan may continue to contradict himself, repeating, exposing his flaws and warts and inconsistencies, nevertheless he knows it, he's aware of it, he understands himself. Consequently this song alleges to denounce his previous position as a singer and writer of protest songs:

Half-wracked prejudice leaped forth
"rip down all hate," I screamed
Lies that life is black and white
Spoke from my skull. I dreamed
Romantic facts of musketeers . . . .

He chides himself for the militant, simplistic anger, the bombastic rhetoric of songs like "Masters of War." " 'We'll meet on edges, soon,' said I. . . ." And he concludes each confession with the repeated refrain:

Ah, but I was so much older then,
I'm younger than that now.

Right. True. But as we listen to this performance, there seems to be an inconsistency. There seems to be a big difference between what Dylan's

JIM MARSHALL

JIM MARSHALL

Late 1964. **Dylan tours England again, this time with a film crew along to make a documentary version of the tour, later released as *Don't Look Back.* One memorable cinema verite scene seems to record the final breakup of Dylan's personal relationship with Joan Baez. Around the same time, Albert Grossman's wife Sally introduces Dylan to her friend Sarah Lowndes, who lives in the Chelsea Hotel with her daughter. To be near her, Dylan also takes an apartment at the Chelsea.**

Above: With Albert Grossman and left: With Phil Ochs, both at Newport, 1964

trying to say and the total feeling that emerges, the stridence and continuing militancy of even this self-denunciation. Is he aware of the contradiction? Is he really turning his back on all that to indulge exclusively in this "other side." In fact, Dylan has continued since 1964 to write political songs, protest songs, mythic apocalyptic songs of greater subtlety and sophistication. The irony of "My Back Pages," good as it is, is that whereas he's congratulating himself for now seeing the light, in that very act he's demonstrating what he's denying; he's delivering yet another didactic absolution, which in time will itself become obsolete. Or as he puts it in the last verse:

Good and bad, I define these terms
Quite clear, no doubt, somehow . . .

And he always will.

"I Don't Believe You" is a bitter song, a lover's sour note on separation, tempered by a lovely Latin melody and rhythm, taunting in its lyrics . . . .

I can be just like you
An' pretend that we never

"Bob—I think that the times they are a-changing. You seem to be in a different kind of bag now, Bob—and I'm worried about it. I saw at Newport how you had somehow lost contact with people. It seemed to me that some of the paraphernalia of fame were getting in your way . . . . Your new songs seem to be all inner-directed now, inner-probing, self-conscious—maybe even a little maudlin or a little cruel on occasion . . . .

I think, in a sense, that we are all responsible for what's been happening to you—and to many other fine young artists. The American Success Machinery chews up geniuses at a rate of one a day and still hungers for more. Unable to produce real art on its own, the establishment breeds creativity in protest against and nonconformity to the System. And then, through notoriety, fast money and status, it makes it almost impossible for the artist to function and grow.

It is a process that must be constantly guarded against and fought. —Irwin Silber

Sing Out! 1964

Right: With Donovan and Mary Travers

JIM MARSHALL

DAVID GAHR

REX FEATURES

Early 1965. **Dylan goes into the studio to produce his fifth album. An outtake of a new song, "Mr. Tambourine Man" is sent to David Crosby of the Byrds. The Byrds record and release an electric, rock 'n' roll single of "Mr. Tambourine Man," which soars up the Top Forty charts and ignites Dylan to explore new possibilities for his own back-up band. Subsequently the new album pulls out all the stops, and Dylan's transition from folk and protest singer to electric rock 'n' roller is nearly complete.**

Photo: With Mike Seeger

have touched.

And whoever said Bob Dylan can't write an interesting and original melody should listen again to this cut.

"Ballad in Plain D" is plain indeed; it's downright nasty, painfully frank, almost more than we want to know about the breakup of Dylan's relationship with a bronze-skinned girl. The girl is Suze Rotolo. Suze and Bob did live together for some time with her mother and her sister Carla. And this starkly autobiographical song does painfully chronicle that byzantine domestic scene and its dissolution: the demise of an important love into backbiting bitterness on all sides. Of all the different, disparate ways Dylan wrote about this incident, this "Ballad" is the most naked and the most unpleasant. The tacky dialogue, the very human, neurotic familial interaction. It's like a soap opera, unkindest to Dylan above all:

Myself, for what I did, I cannot be excused,
The changes I was going through can't even be used,
For the lies that I told her in hopes not to lose
The could-be dream-lover of my lifetime.

Candid stuff. It's by no means his greatest writing, but what catharsis! "And I in my armor, turning about." Dylan doesn't need an analyst to talk to; he works it out all in public, taking off his psychic clothes right there in front of us all.

Once again, Dylan has selected the final song on this album to sum it all up. "It Ain't Me Babe" is loosely based on the old folksong made famous by Burl Ives. . . . Remember?

Go way from my window, go way from my door
Go way, way, way from my bedside . . . and bother me no more.

In Dylan's version, however, he turns a lover's farewell into something far more meaningful: a kind of existential declaration of independence. He's not only high-tailin' it away from whatever woman this is meant for, but from us, his adoring audience, as well:

You say you're lookin' for someone
Never weak but always strong . . .
Someone to open each and every door . . .
But it ain't me, babe . . .
It ain't me you're lookin' for, babe.

"No, no, no," he cries. And what a powerful no, what a chant, what a prayer. And that's the point of this album. I'm not what you want, Dylan says. I'm not your prophet-hero, I'm not your leader, I'm not a public-politico-protestor. I'm not-not-not, leave me alone!

Dylan's performance is so strong, so convincing, that we want to identify with him. The song becomes yet another sort of anthem, a personal proclamation of freedom: leave *us* alone, *we* won't be chained down either. Each of us can recognize ourselves in this situation: in relation to our parents, teachers, lovers, in reaction to the expectations of convention. It's not *us,* either, whatever you expected or wanted or needed, we can't provide it: "No, no, no . . ."

On his liner notes for this album, Dylan writes:

I know no answers an no truth
for absolutely no soul alive . . .
so go joshua
go fit your battle
i have t go t the woods
for a while
i hope you understand . . .

Dylan couldn't get to those woods for a while longer, but the intention is clear. This album has attempted to back off from the near-caricature image of the "protest" singer deliberately constructed in *The Times They Are A-Changin',* and to a degree, it has succeeded. We are convinced Dylan isn't as simple as anything we've thought of him so far, that he's still searching, and that there's no telling where his quest will lead.

JIM MARSHALL

"I had heard the Beatles in New York when they first hit. Then, when we were driving through Colorado we had the radio on and eight of the top ten songs were Beatles songs . . . They were doing things nobody was doing. Their chords were outrageous, just outrageous, and their harmonies made it all valid. You could only do that with other musicians. Even if you're playing your own chords you had to have other people playing with you. That was obvious. And it started me thinking about other people . . . . I knew they were pointing the direction of where music had to go . . . . It was outrageous, and I kept it in my mind. You see, there was a lot of hypocrisy all around, people saying it had to be either folk or rock. But I knew it didn't have to be like that. I dug what the Beatles were doing, and always kept it in mind from back then." —Bob Dylan

To Anthony Scaduto in *Dylan: An Intimate Biography* © 1971, 1973 by Anthony Scaduto

ACCEPTING CHAOS

CL 2328

COLUMBIA

Bob Dylan

Bringing It All Back Home

Bringing It All Back Home

Columbia Stereo CS9128 or Mono CL2328. Produced by Tom Wilson. Released March 1965. Subterranean Homesick Blues, She Belongs to Me, Maggie's Farm, Love Minus Zero/No Limit, Outlaw Blues, On the Road Again, Bob Dylan's 115th Dream; Mr. Tambourine Man, Gates of Eden, It's Alright, Ma (I'm only Bleeding), It's All Over Now, Baby Blue. *All by Bob Dylan.*

Look out. The front-cover art on this fifth album is positively *weeeeird.* It's back to full color again, but there's that *distortion,* that kinda psychedelic *blur* circling the picture, framing a strange collection of *meaningful objects* strewn across our vision. Clearly these are *symbols,* fraught with meaning that's kind of difficult to decipher: Lyndon Johnson on the cover of *Time* magazine, a fallout shelter sign, albums by Lotte Lenya, Robert Johnson, the Impressions, and back there tucked behind a cushion nearly out of sight, why, that's Bob's last album, *Another Side,* nearly obscured by a cool-looking scarlet lady with a cigarette (it's Sally Grossman). And there's Bob Dylan himself, staring out at us so intensely from the center of the bull's-eye, dressed in black with a cat in his lap: wired, coiled, and ready to pounce, so menacing, so dark and mysterious, so ready to blow the damn fuse and explode right out of the frame.

The photo was no accident. He's telling us: here it comes, get out of the way. No more Mr. Niceguy, there are all these things buzzing around in my head like a hundred thousand volts of red-hot, white-steel energy. It's an overload! It's got to get out, so brace yourself. I'm gonna give it to you like it *is*.

The title, *Bringing It All Back Home,* accurately describes Dylan's intention: to escape the folk and protest music and return to his first love: rock 'n' roll. To bring back or withdraw his creativity and psychic energy from the public posture of folk purist or political dissident and return to his center, his home, his heart, the music he grew up with: rock 'n' roll. In fact the break is not so clean cut or simple. This is not completely a rock album but rather a transitional collection with some big electric sound as well as some acoustic compositions on Side Two. But the album is a departure, and it's amazing to consider how it shocked and outraged fans and critics at the time.

We know now that Dylan had played rock 'n' roll in high school, that he never really stopped loving it since, that in 1963 he recorded a few rock 'n' roll cuts ("Corrina" and "Mixed-up Confusion"), which were overlooked and poorly distributed. In 1965, however, Dylan's open embrace of electric rock was seen as some kind of radical change, as a "sellout" to commercial pressures, as an artificial descent into the mire of mass-market music and—most of all—as a betrayal of The Movement's political idealism. Dylan was attacked for turning his back on the revolution. Wealth and fame, they said, had lured him into cheap complacency, and by singing pop music he had committed "class betrayal," alienating above all the intellectuals and liberals who had been his very first fans.

What these lefties failed to realize was that rock 'n' roll has always been revolutionary music. Rock 'n' roll began to emerge from the black community in the late 1950's, striking a rebellious nerve in middle-class white kids and emerging in the sixties as the quintessential revolutionary music of individual revolt. Looking back now, historians can date the real youth rebellion from the earliest Alan Freed rock 'n' roll riots in the 1950's. And whereas academic folk purists turned up their noses at the time, rock 'n' roll nevertheless became the first real mass political weapon of that generation, the best way to say *"No!"* to parents, teachers, the government, to express the revolutionary energy of sex and violence and personal rebellion.

Dylan knew this. He had always

March 1965. *Bringing It All Back Home* is released. Though it alienates some of his former admirers, it sells better and faster than any of his previous albums, becoming his first million-dollar record.

DAVID GAHR

Photo: With Bob Siggins of Charles River Valley Boys

May 1965. Dylan writes and records "Like a Rolling Stone," produced by Tom Wilson, with Mike Bloomfield on electric guitar, Al Kooper on organ and piano, and Bobby Gregg on drums. Released in June as a single, it rises quickly up the charts, hitting number one on some Top Forty lists by early August. His first pop single hit, "Like a Rolling Stone" has a tremendous impact and is thought by many fans to be the greatest song he's ever written.

known it. He repressed this aspect of his personality and his music, arriving in New York to ride the crest of folk and protest music. That *was* what was happening. Now, in 1965, things had changed. Kennedy was dead. Black people had taken over their own civil-rights movement, expelling the white liberals. Lyndon Johnson was President. Disillusion was in the air. It was becoming clear that the simple-minded solutions of the early sixties just weren't going to happen. Marijuana, LSD, and other drugs were becoming more widespread. People were fed up with trying to change the world and began to think about changing *themselves*. So there *was* a real revolution going on, in fact, and rock was its beat. Dylan, contrary to the opinion of some, was right on the mark.

In any case, there's a whole lot of new things going on in this album, a sense of urgency and change and frenzy, of speed and anger. A brilliant, brittle sort of static. On the back of the album is a photo of Dylan slumped in a chair, exhausted, a cigarette in one hand, the other hand covering his eyes. His head is bowed, and a young woman is caressing it, running her fingers through his hair, massaging his skull, soothing, comforting. In another shot we see him grinning devilishly, dressed as a Mad Hatter, surrounded by a crush of fans.

DAVID GAHR

Dylan was accelerating at a blinding speed: writing, performing, recording, concertizing, touring, traveling constantly. It was a period of tremendous productivity but also of huge expenditures of energy. And it shows. There's a crazy manic flavor to this album that's amost out of control. On his liner notes, he writes:

I accept chaos. i am not sure whether it accepts me . . . I am about t sketch You a picture of what goes on around here sometimes. tho I don't understand too well myself what's really happening. i do know that we're all gonna die someday. . . .

No doubt the quick, incredible turns his life had taken both delighted and bewildered him, spinning him around. But through it all, his accomplishment was to produce more and more good music.

"Subterranean Homesick Blues" opens the album with a bang. It's an electric, big-sound, full-band song—with a vengeance. At first hearing, it sounds like cacophonic static. Dylan couldn't have chosen a better vehicle than this murky, echoing, muddy, big-beat hoedown to let everyone know what he was up to. A very harsh song, sung in a nasal, edgy voice full of speed and paranoia. "Look out, kid," it warns in a panegyric to adolescent rebelliousness:

Ah get born, keep warm
Short pants, romance, learn to dance
Get dressed, get blessed
Try to be a success
Please her, please him, buy gifts
Don't steal, don't lift
Twenty years of schoolin'
And they put you on the day shift. . . .

The punk as political rebel, ducking the man in the trench coat, the D.A., the army, stay away, be-ware. What a catalog of warnings, highlighted by some prophetic lines:

Look out kid
Don't matter what you did . . .
Keep a clean nose
Watch the plain clothes
You don't need a weather man
To know which way the wind blows.

Is there anyone who doesn't remember how that line gave a new name to a militant splinter group of the Students for a Democratic Society? The

DAVID GAHR

> As composer, interpreter, most of all as lyricist, Dylan has made a revolution. He expanded folk idiom into a rich, figurative language, grafted literary and philosophical subtleties onto the protest song, revitalized folk vision by rejecting proletarian and ethnic sentimentality, then all but destroyed pure folk as a contemporary form by merging it with pop.—Ellen Willis

DAVID GAHR

Weathermen. Bombs in the name of Dylan. And don't forget:

Look out kid
You're gonna get hit. . . .
Don't follow leaders
Watch the parkin' meters.

What could be clearer. A nearly overt message to his would-be followers. How could anyone deny or overlook the political message of this song: nihilistic, iconoclastic, idiosyncratic, a spit-clear revolutionary position.

"She Belongs to Me" is a nasty, bitter tribute to a woman who doesn't belong to him at all, a woman who walked out without a backward glance. The line "She don't look back" was used as the title for the Pennybacker film documentary of Dylan's tour of England (in which there's a scene where Joan Baez does walk quietly out the door). In any case, Dylan sings this in a low sometimes resonant voice, mellow but often tinged with anger. Jesus, what did this lady do to him? She seems to inflict such pain, he convinces us that such an admirable creature is also a monster.

DAVID GAHR

"Maggie's Farm" reaffirms the revolutionary personal posture of this album. As in "Subterranean Homesick Blues" it's a noisy, electric, rock/protest/nay-saying diatribe of individual rebellion. I *won't* do this and I *won't* do that.

No, I ain't gonna work on Maggie's
farm no more.
Well, I try my best
To be just like I am,

***July 25, 1965.* Dylan appears at the Newport Folk Festival wearing a black leather jacket and high-heel boots. He's carrying an electric guitar and is backed up by the huge electric rock cacophony of the Paul Butterfield Blues Band. Some of the folk festival audience is incensed with anger, and boos; others complain vociferously that Dylan can't be heard against the overamplification of the electric band. The performance dissolves in conflict and confusion.**

Photos from Newport 1965 with Mike Bloomfield on lead guitar and Al Kooper on keyboard

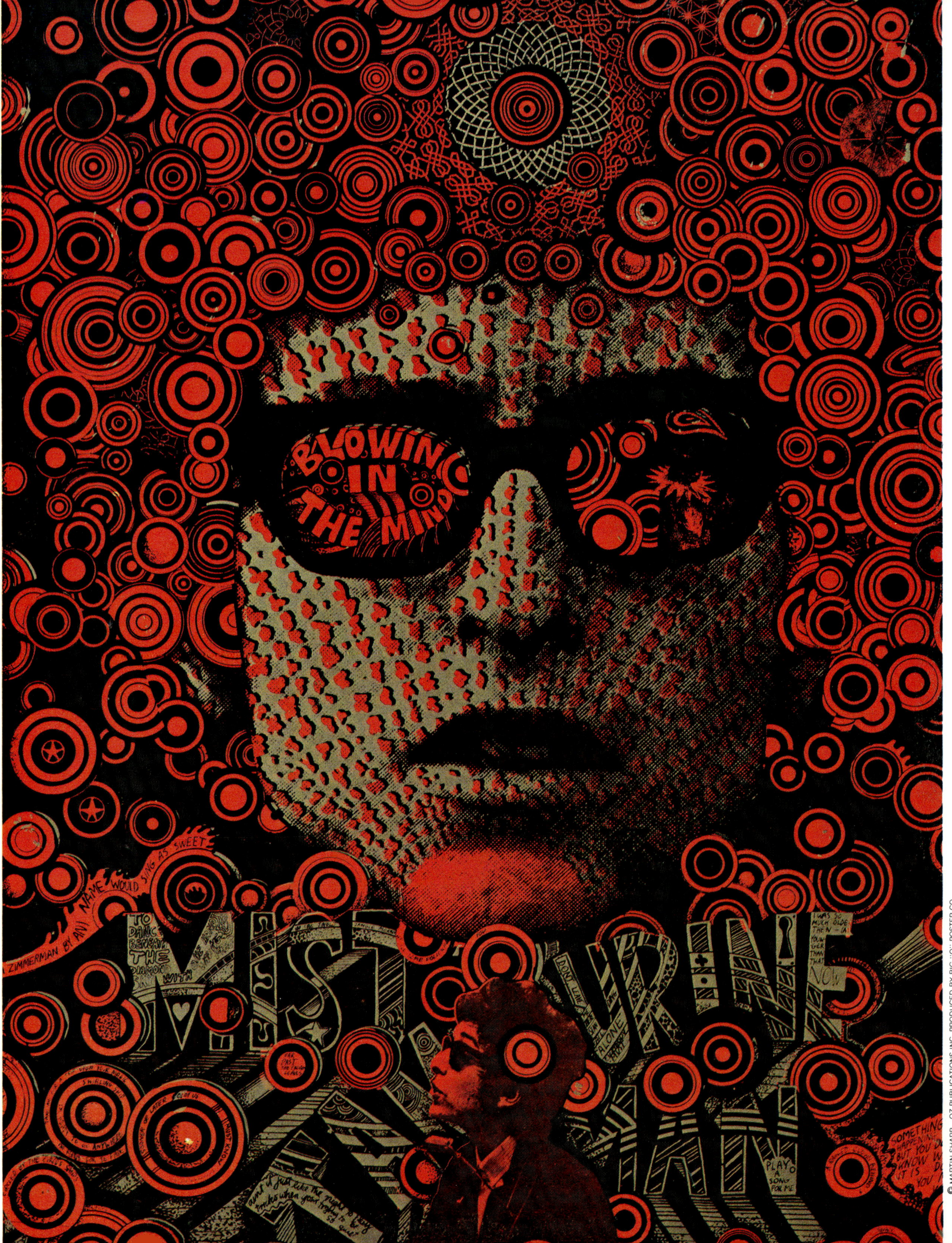
BLOWING IN THE MIND
ZIMMERMAN BY ANY NAME WOULD SING AS SWEET

> "It doesn't matter what kind of nasty names people invent for the music. It could be called arsenic music, or perhaps Phaedra music. I don't think that such a word as folk-rock has anything to do with it. And folk music is a word I can't use. Folk music is a bunch of fat people. I have to think of all this as traditional music. Traditional music is based on hexagrams. It comes about from legends, Bibles, plagues, and it revolves around vegetables and death."—Bob Dylan

But everybody wants you
To be just like them.
They sing while you slave and I just
get bored. . . .

Like the other electrified numbers of the first side of this album, this song isn't strictly speaking "hard" rock. Dylan plays his ax as if it were acoustic. But there's Bruce Langhorne and a stalwart group of rock musicians flailing away behind him, the beat is there, and the overall muddy effect provides a wall of sound that turns the trick. It's also interesting to note that Dylan is escaping in this song not only from Maggie but from all her relatives as well: her brother, her Pa, her Ma, the whole family. Dylan sees his women friends in the context of their family, particularly as the children of their mothers and fathers. It's as if he wants not just a lover, but a total relationship with the whole family. This preoccupation is characteristic of Dylan's central belief that the family is the structure within which one finds love, stability, and ultimately salvation. It's a critical part of his continuing quest, this belief and this need, a source of constant striving and struggle and disappointment.

"Love Minus Zero/No Limit" is an idealized vision of budding love, somewhat unconvincingly thrown away. . . . In contrast, "Outlaw Blues" opens with a terrific Chuck Berry-style riff, which continues throughout as a solid backbeat for this most authentic rocker on the record. In "On the Road Again," Dylan is once again

Opposite: Martin Sharp's poster from "Get On Down"

leaving his lover *and* her eccentric family. Dylan himself is the straight man in this fantasy. Everyone else is weird. Crazy. Madness is seeping through and surrounding him all through this album. People and events are assaulting Dylan, who tries to remain passive, confused, even innocent in his naiveté.

Similarly, "Bob Dylan's 115th Dream" is a fascinating, bizarre tale of paranoia. Seems like everyone is out to get him as he sails in on the *Pequod/Mayflower* with Captain Arab/Ahab and actually discovers America. This dream is typical of the multi-leveled,

DAVID GAHR

surrealistic, droll tales Dylan wrote during this period, full of word plays, twisted reality, druggy visions. There's a wonderful moment at the beginning of this cut when Dylan starts off briskly without realizing that his band hasn't come in with its accompaniment. Dylan laughs. Dylan breaks up! And what a laugh: high, rich, open, full, free, and funny. Dylan himself insisted it be left on the track, setting an "open mike" precedent that many artists have followed since, hoping to capture such spontaneous (but appealing) mistakes. And when Dylan starts off again, this time with his back-up group behind him, you can tell he feels better, his voice is fuller, happier, richer, and more relaxed. This accident resulted in a different song and probably a better one.

On the second side of this album, Dylan drops the back-up and returns to a strictly acoustic accompaniment,

"I have watched with fascination the meteoric rise of this American idol and I am still unable to see in him anything other than a youth of mediocre talent. Only a completely non-critical audience, nourished on the watery pap of pop music, could have fallen for such tenth-rate drivel. "But the poetry?" What poetry? The cultivated illiteracy of his topical songs of the embarrassing fourth-grade schoolboy attempts at free verse? The latter reminds me of elderly female schoolteachers clad in Greek tunics rolling hoops across lawns at weekend theater schools . . . . [Dylan] exemplifies contemporary American songwriting, a movement where journalism is more important than art, where flabby sentimentality and shrill self-pity take the place of passion. — Ewan MacColl"

In *Sing Out!* 1965

"Dylan has sold out to God. That is to say, his command was to spread his beauty as wide as possible. It was an artistic challenge to see if great art can be done on a juke box. And he proved it can.—Allen Ginsberg"

1966

"Bob Dylan has become a pawn in his own game. He has ceased his Quest for a Universal Sound and has settled for a liaison with the music trade's Top Forty Hit Parade. . . . If necessary, he'll sing songs he repudiated. For example, he sang many songs in England he no longer sings here because the English audience is two years behind his American image. Next year, he'll be writing rhythm-and-blues songs when they get high on the charts. The following year, the Polish polka will make it, and then he'll write them, too. By then, he'll be so mired in the popularity charts that he'll be safe enough for the State Department to have them send him to entertain troops at whatever battlefront we're on at the time. . . . I don't think it's worth it, Bob. If you don't watch out, you'll become commercial.—Israel G. Young"

In *Sing Out!* 1965

opening with the classic "Mr. Tambourine Man," one of the most explicit drug songs Dylan has produced and probably the best song ever written on the subject.

Though I know that evenin's empire
has returned into sand,
Vanished from my hand,
Left me blindly here to stand but
still not sleeping.
My weariness amazes me, I'm branded
on my feet,
I have no one to meet
And the ancient empty street's too
dead for dreaming

What a brilliant evocation of the drug experience. What wonderfully accurate images: "In the jingle jangle morning . . . my senses have been stripped . . . take me disappearin' through the smoke rings of my mind . . ." Strung out, desperate to get off, Dylan's melody has all the yearning and plaintiveness of the pleasure-seeking lotus-eater. The words have become gospel, through this and many other famous recordings, most notably the electric, rock and roll version by The Byrds.

"Gates of Eden" is an update of Dylan's continuing apocalyptic vision. In this very long, biblical sermon, all that lies outside the gates is a brutish nightmare. Within lies paradise. It's black and white, an escapist fantasy: from life on earth, from his lover, from words themselves.

And I try to harmonize with songs
The lonesome sparrow sings . . .
At times I think there are no words
But these to tell what's true
And there are no truths outside the
Gates of Eden.

But Dylan cannot escape words and despite his avowed intention in "My Back Pages"—he cannot avoid his predeliction to find the "answer." In this attempt, he seems especially depressed and desperate and crazy. Nothing seems to make sense. The only hope for salvation is in the mythic past, or perhaps, if we're lucky, in the next world.

"It's Alright, Ma (I'm Only Bleeding)" carries on this theme of desperation, bad craziness, alienation, isolation. Dylan seems to be having a really hard time: sighing, crying, dying. Nobody knows and nobody cares and nobody understands. The descending chord progressions are so gloomy, so doomy, so saturated with suffering. Such a grim seven-and-a-half minute dirge, this nightmarish "thought-dream!" Like a lot of cuts on this album, it is not exactly fun to hear.

JIM MARSHALL

He's hanging by a thread but he *will* survive. "It's alright, Ma, it's life, and life only." Life is nearly, but not quite, impossible. I'm bleeding but I can make it, he says: aloof, isolated, outside, hardened to the craziness and suffering and despair around him, for which he seems to express some self-protective contempt. Again, there are some memorable lines, including:

The hollow horn plays wasted words
Proves to warn
That he not busy being born
Is busy dying.

And it's all directed at Ma, like so many of his desperate, deepest songs.

The last track on this album is, appropriately, "It's All Over Now, Baby Blue," and it reaffirms the strident, grim tone of the previous cuts. Death is just around the corner. Death permeates this entire second side of the album. The first side is full of nay-saying rebellion. But after the walls have been torn down, the false images burned, and freedom declared, only death remains. In "Tambourine Man" drugs are the escape; in "Gates of Eden" he offers the faint hope of paradise *after* life; he bleeds for his mother, and now in his final farewell of the album: he DIES! The song is about saying good-bye to a lover, but the effect of his delivery says so much more about the singer himself. On the one hand his singing is strong and definite and confident. On the other hand he expresses despair, anger, and craziness. This album portrays an ecstatic nightmare of horrors spinning around him while he hangs by his fingertips from the cliff, WRITING about it all, using it, getting it all down. And wait, we *can*—as he says at the end of this song—"strike another match, go start anew . . ." even though "it's all over now, Baby Blue." Thanks for that faint encouragement.

Of course it's only a record, a *tour de force* by a brilliant actor. We know now how well he actually survived. This album was a stunning success, his best-selling record to date. From this time on Dylan had the option to play alone *or* with a band. And the four songs on Side Two brilliantly convey the sense of anguish and confusion and violence and speed he was experiencing at the time, his star higher than he had ever expected, his fame and wealth increasing precipitously, his life crazy beyond belief.

"I was playing rock 'n' roll when I was 13 and 14 and 15, but I had to quit when I was 16 or 17 because I couldn't make it that way, the image of the day was Frankie Avalon or Fabian, or this whole athletic supercleanness bit, you know, which if you didn't have that, you couldn't make any friends. — Bob Dylan"

Interview with Joseph Haas, Chicago *Daily News,* 1965

August 27, 1965. **Dylan fills the Forest Hills Tennis Stadium in Queens. This time his back-up band includes his new friends Robbie Robertson and Levon Helm of the group then known as the Hawks and later as The Band. This time the audience is less surprised and less hostile to Dylan's new image and musical identity. By his third appearance as a hard rock 'n' roller in Carnegie Hall, a month later, most of the fuss is over. Dylan by this time has disillusioned some people and others from now on will mistrust his chameleonlike identity transplants. But he's produced great rock 'n' roll art and rightfully won a huge number of new fans. Hundreds and thousands of young people around the world are now tuned in to Dylan's manic visions and moralistic teachings. The pressure to produce, the demands of personal appearances and exhausting concert tours, the stress and momentum increase precipitously as Dylan — moving very quickly and wasting no time — goes into the studio with a new producer to lay down the tracks for the album to be known as *Highway 61 Revisited.***

Photo: With the Hawks

BOB DYLAN HIGHWAY 61 REVISITED

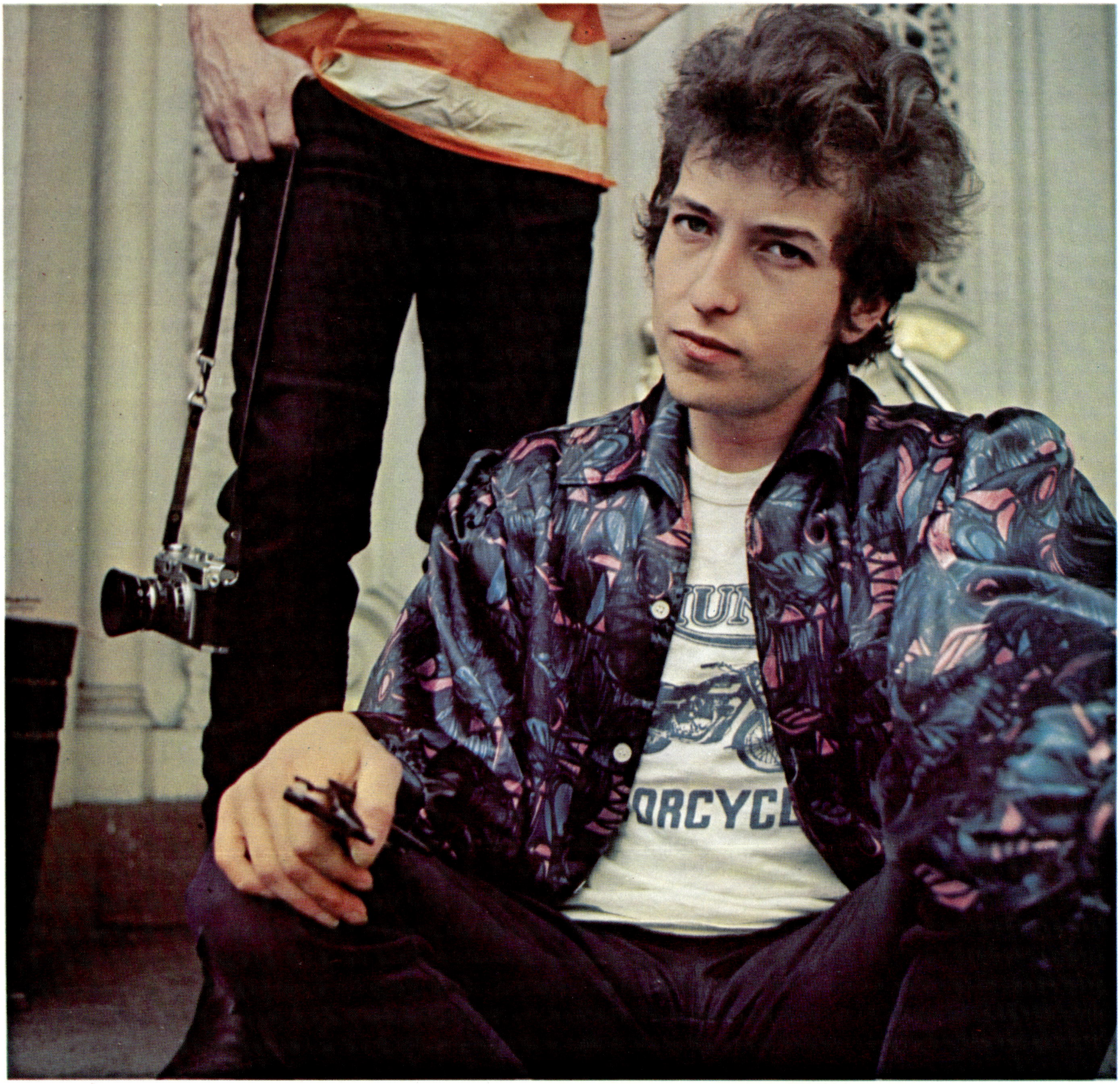

Highway 61 Revisited

Columbia Stereo KCS 9189 or Mono CL 2389. Produced by Bob Johnston, except Like a Rolling Stone, *produced by Tom Wilson. Released August 1965.* Like a Rolling Stone, Tombstone Blues, It Takes a Lot to Laugh, It Takes a Train to Cry, From a Buick 6, Ballad of a Thin Man; Queen Jane Approximately, Highway 61 Revisited, Just Like Tom Thumb's Blues, Desolation Row. *All written by Bob Dylan.*

The cover shot for this album is outrageous. Bob Dylan dressed in psychedelic punk-rock clothes (and this was only 1965), his shiny blue-and-purple shirt unbuttoned, his Triumph Motorcycle T-shirt peeking through. He's leaning back a little, sunglasses in his right hand. His eyes are level but a little weak and squinty, as if they've been mostly covered up for a while—they're watery and rheumy and not too comfortable in the light. His mouth is pursed, defiant, annoyed, angry even. Shades of Jimmy Dean and Marlon Brando. Tough guy. Rock star. That's the pose. Only the soulful Jewish face, both soft and tough, sensitive and serious, sad but self-deprecating—reminds us that it's yet another costume, and this, too, shall pass.

Meanwhile, this is Dylan's first 100 percent rock 'n' roll album, with a clear, rich, well-engineered sound and a terrific back-up band which included Michael Bloomfield on guitar, Al Kooper on piano and organ, Charley McCoy on guitar, Russ Savakus on bass, and several other fine musicians. There's a lot of energy on this record: driving, burning, speeding, it's focused in feelings of bitterness and revenge. Actually, the underlying theme of this album is defiance and *revenge.* Dylan seems so angry, so tired of having to explain, so mad at lots of people . . . or is it that he is just plain *mad.* Loony. If he was moving fast before, back on *Another Side* or *Bringing It All Back Home,* he's moving ten times that blinding rate of speed by this album. A glimpse of this insane frenzy can be seen in the Pennybaker documentary of his English tour, *Don't Look Back,* which is a kind of black comedy version of *Hard Day's Night.* Dylan does not seem to be enjoying himself very much during this period, and his music shows it. Why? The pressures of fame, the distortions of hostile media, the fickleness of friends and fans, particularly in their misunderstanding of his rock conversion, the lack of peace or quiet or rest on the road . . . .

People who'd never have listened during the blue-jeans and work-shirt days were now enormously turned on by his electric, hard-driving, violent songs of rebellion. In fact, Dylan was doing more to revolutionize and influence American society now, singing rock 'n' roll, than he had ever been able to accomplish as a folk-music protest singer. More individual, more personal, Dylan's songs nonetheless

November 22, 1965. **Bob Dylan marries Sarah Lowndes in a civil ceremony attended only by close friends. This marriage is kept secret from the public until the following February.**

Right after his wedding, Dylan launches a series of exhausting, whirlwind concert tours across the United States and around the world. His albums and singles are selling millions of copies — three of his records are on the charts. Bob Dylan is as well known and more influential than the Beatles or the Rolling Stones. Bob Dylan is a bona fide superstar.

JIM MARSHALL

JIM MARSHALL

Left: With Robbie Robertson, Michael McClure, Allen Ginsburg and Lawrence Ferlenghetti in San Francisco

He is accused in some circles of selling out for money and commercial popularity. But Dylan's new identity as a rocker is no more of a deliberate pose than his previous incarnation as a folksinger. His electrification is consistent with both his musical background and his uncanny sense of the appropriate musical style needed to express what everyone is feeling at the time. Rage and self-centering nihilism are widespread in the middle sixties, but people are turning on to the big beat. There may be disillusion in the public arena, but deep down on the inside, folks are getting into the rhythm.

The Beatles had begun to legitimize rock among students and the intelligentsia. Dylan takes it further, using rock 'n' roll to express complex personal visions, parables with messages like a sermon—moralizing, judgmental—poetic epiphanies of love, despair, angst, and... madness. Dylan does seem to be nearly mad during this period of intense creativity and success, continuing travel, and hysterical adulation. And it's harder for Dylan than for a star like Elvis Presley because Dylan writes songs that make people think he has the Answer. At this point people treat Dylan more like the Messiah than a superstar. The pressure makes Dylan uncomfortable.

> "Dylan is no apostle of the electronic age. Rather, he is a fifth-columnist from the past, shaped by personal and political non-conformity, by blues and modern poetry. He has imposed his commitment to individual freedom (and its obverse, isolation) on the hip passivity of pop culture, his literacy on an illiterate music. He has used the publicity machine to demonstrate his belief in privacy. His songs and public role are guides to survival in the world of the image, the cool, and the high. And in coming to terms with that world, he has forced it to come to terms with him."—Ellen Willis
>
> In *Cheetah,* © 1967 by Ellen Willis

FRED W. McDARRAH

FRED W. McDARRAH

have stimulated self-understanding, change and revolution in each of us, for example:

"Like a Rolling Stone," the first cut on this album and perhaps the most famous song Dylan has ever written, works on several levels. It's a hard-driving, quintessential rock 'n' roll song. The music, the beat, the effect of his performance: it's electric. No one else has been able to sing this song, either, only Dylan. It's the Heartbreak Hotel, the Tutti Frutti of his career—you want to jump out of your seat when you hear it. It's also a vicious, nasty song of hostility and revenge against a woman, "Miss Lonely," who's been riding quite high, seems to have left him along the way, and is now heading for a big fall on her own. Dylan could have written this song to Suze Rotolo or to Joan Baez or to a part of himself. It's a song any of us could sing to ourselves, since finally it's a song about our own separation, about the fundamental isolation each of us must face:

How does it feel?
Ahhhhhh, How does it feel?
To be on your own?
With no direction ***home!***
Like a complete unknown
Like a rolling stone!

Dylan punches and hammers those words right into the marrow of our bones. It hurts because we know it's true for all of us. She's alone and he's alone and we're alone, too. We've all felt this way: the spite and madness and anger, the sense of disappointment in a loved one's behavior, the failed expectations and above all the realization that we can't always depend on anyone but ourselves. Elsewhere—in other songs—Dylan has been able to remind us of the connections we do have with others, the possibilities and occasional rewards of love, contact, communication. But this song shows us the dark side; it's a devastating harangue about existential alienation. Maybe we thought we could get together, maybe we did get together—for a while—but we can't anymore and it's over. The combination of words and music and dramatic performance on this beautifully produced recording is extraordinary and deservedly celebrated.

"Tombstone Blues" is chanted over a solid rock beat, a talking blues, Western style, whose chorus echoes a recurrent theme of many Dylan songs, the breakup of the family:

Mama's in the fac'try
She ain't got no shoes
Daddy's in the alley
He's lookin' for the fuse
I'm in the streets
With the tombstone blues.

Dylan has often said he never really thinks much about the ideas or points to be made in his songs but more or less just strings the words together so they sound good. A phrase, a line, a rhyme that seems to work. It may not be as simple as all that, but it's easy to believe that he did write a song like "Tombstone Blues" in such a spontaneous, pragmatic way, stringing out the Dada, nightmare visions, the Hollywood flashes, the biblical metaphors of this epic:

Now I wish I could give Brother Bill
his great thrill
I would set him in chains at the top
of the hill
Then send out for some pillars and
Cecil B. DeMille
He could die happily ever after.

"It takes a Lot to Laugh, It Takes a Train to Cry" strikes a happier chord. Dylan really seems to enjoy playing with this band, getting down and having a ball. He sings this song beautifully; in fact, his singing on this entire album is some of the best he's ever done. This number is a bit more hopeful toward relationships: the moon looks good, his gal looks fine. There's another conciliatory line, reminiscent of "All I Really Want to Do":

Well, I wanna be your lover, baby,
I don't want to be your boss.

Can you believe it this time, ladies? Sound more convincing? Maybe it's the lovely chord progression and the good Latin beat.

"Ballad of a Thin Man" has been interpreted as a put-down addressed to some square nitwit, a precursor to the Beatles "No-Where Man." The chorus has become famous and oft-repeated as a political slogan:

Because something is happening here
But you don't know what it is
Do you, Mister Jones?

As if Mr. Jones were the archetypal parent or teacher or older establishment official bewildered by the whirling tides of change. The music hammers away at this poor fellow with a percussive piano and a declining chord progression guaranteed to nail you to the wall. But who *is* the thin man with the pencil, the freak who's read all of F. Scott Fitzgerald and should be made to wear earphones? Well, it could be Dylan himself, wouldn't you say? It's Dylan, after all, who's taken a pseudonym. And it's Dylan who's bewildered, who really wants to know what's going on behind all this confusion.

You raise up your head
And you ask, "Is this where it is?"
And somebody points to you and says
"It's his."
And you say "What's mine?"
And somebody else says, "Where
what is?"
And you say, "Oh my God
Am I here all alone?"

What a crushing minidrama of existential angst. And it can be taken as a dialogue Dylan's having with *himself.* It may be an adolescent put-down on a superficial level, but it's also self-examination, even self-contempt.

"Queen Jane Approximately" says, "Come see me when you're tired of your bullshit," plain and simple. The rhythm is lilting, almost Latin. The singing is easygoing. But the message is yet another act of revenge.

When your mother sends back all your
invitations
And your father to your sister he
explains
That you're tired of yourself and all
of your creations
Won't you come see me, Queen Jane?

Not exactly the sort of invitation anyone is likely to accept. But hold it, just who is it that's really getting tired of himself and all his creations? This song has a double edge: on one level it, too, could be about Dylan himself. Perhaps his saving grace throughout this nasty series of songs is his ambivalence, his own identification with the subject of his scorn.

The song "Highway 61 Revisited" is an honorable tribute to the American road, the same road Jack Kerouac and Neal Cassady drove across so many times. "Highway 61" is a witty, tongue-in-cheek celebration of that funky American metaphor: the cement-and-asphalt highway, with its gasoline stains and a stripe down the middle. It's all out there on this road, whatever you want to see, whatever you want to do: there's food and shelter and hot sex, war, God himself . . . just put up some bleachers and watch the parade go by. The circus metaphor is well-conveyed by a slide-whistle whooping up and down the scale between verses. "Highway 61" runs straight up and down the middle of America, linking, holding together, magnetically attracting everyone from Abraham to the Rovin' Gambler. You can get anything, see anything,

FRED W. McDARRAH

leave anything, anything goes on the great American highway. It's silly, it's awful, it's pop, it's the romance of the driver, alone in his car, watching it all go by—it's rock 'n' roll.

"Just Like Tom Thumb's Blues" is a sloshy, laid-back, druggy song about Dylan "lost in the rain in Juarez." Analysts have been quick to pounce on this reference to "rain" or heroin (now known more commonly as "snow"), and there's little doubt what this song's about.

I started out on burgundy
But soon hit the harder stuff
Everybody said they'd stand
behind me
When the game got rough
But the joke was on me
There was nobody even there to call
my bluff. . . .

Dylan has spoken about his use of drugs during this period. Uppers to keep him going on the road, alcohol and cigarettes to calm down, no doubt he experimented with all sorts of stuff. You get the sense Dylan is very tired; all this has been more than he bargained for, and he's taking drugs as a buffer. Unhappily, the drugs have also isolated him, boxing him into himself, making him feel even more separate, alone, and probably a little paranoid. But he's hip to it; he understands and he's ready to blow the whistle:

I'm going back to New York City
I do believe I've had enough. . . .

There's been rumor and speculation about Dylan's use of drugs. One critic has said that Dylan's been a helpless addict for years. Nonsense! Like a lot of us, he's dabbled and experimented and gone through phases. But no one can produce as much as he has and survive for so long if he's an addict. Dylan's just too healthy, too smart, too self-protective for that. . . .

The last cut on this album, "Desolation Row," is a kind of flip side to "Highway 61." Instead of the up-beat, pop-culture highway of life, this song portrays the interior journey; it's about Dylan's intimate reactions to all the external stimuli of his life: with humor and anguish and a very Jewish sense of paradox, of horror as well as the ecstasy of it all. In this all-out Dada *tour de force,* Dylan cleverly makes his metaphors and symbols, eclectically drawing on mystic references to the Bible, literature, pop culture, and politics. He chides Einstein, Ezra Pound, and T.S. Eliot—wryly, affectionately, competitively, as if to bring down gods and false angels such as himself. It's all an act, he seems to be saying; don't take it too seriously, folks. Once in a while the words to this song seem a slave to rhyme. Do they have obscure potential significance or do they just fit? What does it all mean? Who knows—it's a sound, a phrase, a line that sounded right.

On the liner notes to this album, Dylan writes, "Lifelessness said when introducing everybody 'go save the world' & 'involvement! that's the issue' & things like that. . . ." Is Dylan saying involvement is lifelessness? Seems so, judging by the nihilism and distance Dylan puts between himself and his material on this album. He's enjoying himself musically. He's a genuine rock 'n' roll star now, really as big as Elvis Presley at this precise moment. But he's disconnected, short-circuited, disattached from the meaning and relationships that had held him down; he's just speeding around like a whirling dervish. How long can he keep it up?

FRED W. McDARRAH

Early 1966.* Dylan's life accelerates to a dazzling but frightening pace, exploding with speed and power and money and drugs. While touring the United States, Australia, Sweden, Denmark, France, and Italy, he also goes into Columbia's Nashville, Tennessee, studios several times to record a whole batch of new songs which are released in May of 1966 as his first double album, *Blonde on Blonde.

C2S 841
COLUMBIA
STEREO
"360 SOUND"

Blonde on Blonde

Columbia C2S841, CS9316, CS9317. Produced by Bob Johnston. Released May 1966. Rainy Day Women #12 & 35, Pledging My Time, Visions of Johanna, One of Us Must Know (Sooner or Later); I Want You, Stuck Inside of Mobile with the Memphis Blues Again, Leopard-Skin Pill-Box Hat, Just Like a Woman; Most Likely You Go Your Way and I'll Go Mine, Temporary Like Achilles, Absolutely Sweet Marie, Fourth Time Around, Obviously Five Believers; Sad Eyed Lady of the Lowlands. *All by Bob Dylan.*

There's no title on the front of this lucky seventh album, a double record that you open up to see the full head-to-thigh portrait in brown of Bob Dylan. He looks so blurry and bleary, stoned, crazy-haired and wasted . . . or is it that the whole photograph is deliberately out of focus? And what's that in tiny white print down there in the crease where the album folds, is *that* the title: *Blonde on Blonde!* Very mysterious. Is that like white on white? Does he mean to be disappearing? Does he mean to be just shimmering, just shining and reflecting on the surface of all things around him?

With this double album, Dylan completes a cycle of his life, during which he has emerged out of nowhere, changing from a scruffy vagabond folksinger to an international rock 'n' roll star—all within five years. The number of great songs he has written during this brief period is extraordinary: "Blowin' in the Wind," "Girl of the North Country," "Hard Rain," "Don't Think Twice," "The Times They Are A-Changin'," "With God on Our Side," "It Ain't Me Babe," "Mr. Tambourine Man," "It's All Over Now, Baby Blue," "Like a Rolling Stone," "Positively Fourth Street." . . . The speed with which he has continuously reinvented himself, the chances he's taken—and when this album came out, he was only twenty-five years old!

There's lots of music on *Blonde on Blonde.* Many good songs, too many for one record, not quite enough, really, for two. Produced by Bob Johnston at the Columbia Recording Studios in Nashville, Tennessee, this recording is blessed with some terrific country-and-western musicians, including Charlie McCoy, Wayne Moss, Kenneth Buttrey, and Al Kooper, too, just for good measure. The band sounds wonderful, and the sessions seem to have been not only productive but fun. Dylan sounds like he's having a very good time.

The first cut sets the tone for many of the thirteen to follow: "Rainy Day Women #12 & 35" is a gas: a stoned-out shouter, a fine song for marching down the street. The music and the high-stepping beat and the vigorous performance are so full of camaraderie, humor, and fun, they contrast sharply with the words which, if read alone, sound like a paranoid fantasy—just the sort of ironic vision one might very well experience when stoned. The double entendre is worth emphasizing: *"Everybody must get stoned!"* Dylan cries out, tongue-in-cheek,

WIDE WORLD PHOTOS

July 29, 1966. **Dylan crashes. At the height of his manic frenzy, Dylan falls off his Triumph 500 motorcycle in a terrible accident near Woodstock, New York. Hospitalized with a concussion and several broken vertebrae in his neck, Dylan is forced to remain in bed for over a month, recuperating slowly while rumors spread that he is permanently brain-damaged, helplessly insane, or dead — another Jesus or James Dean struck down in his prime.**

In fact, Dylan's enforced convalescence is a blessing in disguise. It forces him to stop. He holds still. He rests and regains his strength. He lives quietly in the woods with his wife and new children and his friend Robbie Robertson and members of The Band. And in this bucolic retreat, he quietly and slowly begins to make some new music, which reflects the radical change in his personal life. He and The Band practice and play around and do some home recordings together in the basement of their house, called The Big Pink, in West Saugerties, New York. Some of this neo-classical jam can be heard on *The Basement Tapes,* first circulated as a bootleg, then officially released in 1975 by Columbia; some more can be heard from The Band alone on their first album *Music from Big Pink.*

JOSEPH STEVENS

Above: Dylan's father, Abraham Zimmerman, with John Sebastian

sounding for all the world like the comic Mr. Kitzel on the old Jack Benny radio show.

Tell ya what, I would not feel so all
alone,
Everybody *must get stoned.*

Getting stoned is fun, but getting stoned is also dangerous. It's not just getting high; it's getting hit by rocks, just like in the Bible. So watch out, folks, they're out to get us: when we're riding in our car or playing the guitar, when we're all alone or just walking home. It's dangerous, and it's scary to take these chances as we march down the street together, like at the Mardi Gras in New Orleans. Dylan sees stones coming at him from all directions and for good reason. But he's confident and good-humored (in *this* song), and the overall effect of the number is irrepressible glee: adolescent, outlaw, damned-if-I-care resolution to take the chance, to welcome the brickbats with the bravos, to lay himself (and us along with him) *out there.*

Lots of love songs on this album. Songs of hope, of starting up something new, like "Pledging My Time":

Now I'm pledging my time to you,
Hopin' you'll come through, too.

Contrasting with songs of lost love, like "Visions of Johanna":

Oh, it's so hard to get on
And these visions of Johanna, they
kept me up past the dawn.

And songs of regret and contrition, like "One of Us Must Know (Sooner or Later)":

I didn't mean to treat you so bad
You shouldn't take it so personal
I didn't mean to make you so sad
You just happened to be there,
that's all . . . .

It's an interesting debate: Dylan admits that he's mistreated this lady, but on the other hand claims she left through no fault of his own and that history will vindicate him:

An I told you, as you clawed out my
eyes
That I never really meant to do you
any harm . . .
Sooner or later, one of us must know
That I really did try to get close to you.

There's been so much speculation about to whom these love songs were written: Is this one for Joan Baez, this one for Suze Rotolo, this one to his wife Sarah? There *are* autobiographical impulses and motivations behind them

REX FEATURES

"*Did taking drugs influence the songs?*
No, not the writing of them, but it did keep me up there to pump 'em out.—Bob Dylan"

In The *Rolling Stone* Interview © 1970 by Straight Arrow Publishers, Inc.

"I'm really not the right person to tramp around the country saving souls . . . . I really don't know what the people who are on the receiving end of these songs think of me, anyway. It's horrible. I'll bet Tony Bennett doesn't have to go through this kind of thing.—Bob Dylan"

The *Playboy* Interview by Nat Hentoff © 1966 by Playboy, Inc.

“The closest I ever got to the sound I hear in my mind was on individual bands in the *Blonde on Blonde* album. It's that thin, that wild mercury sound. It's metallic and bright gold, with whatever that conjures up. That's my particular sound. I haven't been able to succeed in getting it all the time. Mostly, I've been driving at a combination of guitar, harmonica and organ, but now I find myself going into territory that has more percussion in it and [pause] rhythms of the soul.—Bob Dylan”

To Ron Rosenbaum in The *Playboy* Interview © Playboy, March 1978

“There was the storm of seeing him
Of watching him act distant and fake a regular heartbeat
Of laughing as the young dada king pulled off his crazy act on the stage
Of seeing three thousand people forgive the unforgivable because his magic came out of a well of small gems and an inexcusable charm—

He put us all on. But mostly he put himself on . . . a bizarre liar, screaming into the electric microphones under the bright bright lights . . . a huge transparent bubble of ego. And I said yes to the sounds of his rage and his band and I listened and heard the words, the pleadings, the nonsense, the denials and I almost drowned in it but came up over and over to call for more . . . and he went ahead hitting hard and steady until he broke his heart in public—and denied it all backstage afterwards—after the show.

Listen, God, look closely after him. He's more fragile than most people and, besides, I love him. . . .
—The Dada King”

From *Daybreak* by Joan Baez, The Dial Press © 1968 by Joan Baez

“Obvious parallels, or ‘‘influences’’—Blake, Whitman, Rimbaud, Celine—share only his approach and identity: the Great Vulgarian, the Magnificent Phonus Balonus. He wrote like a word-drunk undergraduate who had beserked himself into genius, the jumbled culture of the war baby—from da Vinci to comic strips, from T. S. Eliot to Charlie Rich—his only tradition. His famous surrealism owes as much to Chuck Berry as to Breton or even Corso. . . . —Robert Christgau”

In *The New York Times* © 1971 The New York Times Co.

all, certainly, but what's important is how Dylan is able to universalize the reactions and feelings so that they have meaning for each of us. He approaches the subject from many different angles, trying to unzip his heart in a most candid manner throughout this cycle of confessionals. When it works, we can recognize and share the whole gamut of emotions.

"I Want You" strikes a more positive note. The tempo is upbeat, the singing is driving and determined. Something new is happening, and this boy does mean to get what he wants:

I wasn't born to lose you.
I want you, I want you,
I want you so bad,
Honey, I want you.

This mood extends to the next song, "Stuck Inside of Mobile with the Memphis Blues Again," a rollicking, good-old down-home country blues song with that memorable title refrain:

Oh, Mama, can this really be the end,
To be stuck inside of Mobile
With the Memphis Blues again.

The madcap joviality of this song, however, is in sharp contrast with the words: Dylan's trapped again, cornered, stuck inside a Dada vision full of nightmarish inversions and terrifying word games:

Mona tried to tell me
To stay away from the train line.
She said that all the railroad men
Just drink up your blood like wine.
An' I said, "oh, I didn't know that,
But then again, there's only one I've
met
An' he just smoked my eyelids
An' punched my cigarette."

Heavy. Yes, one could write a Ph.D. thesis on that stanza with all its multileveled, surrealistic, cosmic meaning. Or maybe it's just a bunch of words strung together in a motel room between sessions to make a deadline. It doesn't matter. This is a playful, witty song, and if it had been cut down to half as long, it might have been an AM Top Forty hit.

The next two numbers return to the theme of revenge. "Leopard-Skin Pill-Box Hat" is another bitter song about breaking up. Dylan mocks his former lover with her silly hat and asks sarcastically if he "can jump on it sometime." This is one of his nastiest efforts, just listen to the venomous jealousy:

Well, I see you got a new boyfriend
You know, I never seen him before
Well, I saw him

For fifteen months, Dylan recuperates in this calm and peaceful atmosphere, rebuilding his body, clearing his head. He luxuriates in the bosom of his family, enjoying the new role of husband and father to his growing family, taking a well-earned rest for the first time in his life. He refuses to make any personal appearances or public statements, and he declines to polish or release any of the music he's been playing around with The Band. Consequently, in order to keep some Bob Dylan product on the market during this hiatus, Columbia assembles a *Greatest Hits* album from previous recordings, including one song, "Positively Fourth Street," which has been previously released only as a single.

***October 1967.* After much deliberation, Dylan visits Nashville to record a carefully selected group of his latest compositions. Working with only three studio musicians, he cuts an album that surprises everyone. He sings in a new voice—a gentler, richer, deeper baritone. The songs sound peaceful and more mellow, the melodies are simple and lyric, the rhythm is soft and muted, the accompaniment low-key and largely acoustic. It's not rock 'n' roll; it's more classic country music—but the words are spiritual, as mystic as ever, and more religious.**

Again, Dylan leaps out in front of his hard-rocking peers, leading the way inward toward a revisionist neo-country style with a genuine pastoral sound and a message full of *faith in God!*

Makin' love to you
You forgot to close the garage door . . . .

Is this the same fellow who wrote so tenderly to Johanna that he did try to get close? What a difficult lover Dylan realizes he is and how well he expresses all the contradictory parts of his passion.

"Just Like a Woman" is even more bitter, more belligerent in its attack. This song is a devastating character assassination, a portrait of a fraud: a woman who lives in a fog of amphetamines, who dresses and fakes and takes and poses as a woman, but who "breaks" like a little girl.

Please don't let on that you knew me
when
I was hungry and it was your world.

"Just Like a Woman" may be the most sardonic, nastiest of all Dylan's put-downs of former lovers. Dylan is saying not just good-bye, but good riddance, and how could I ever have been so dumb or thirsty or blind as to have been fooled by you? It's the pits, the rock bottom sentiments of postseparation bitterness.

Yes, "I'm gonna let you pass," Dylan vows in "Most Likely You Go Your Way (and I'll Go Mine)." Again, he feels justified. He's sure that "time will tell just who fell and who's been left behind . . . ." A tough, speedy number with a good beat, Dylan sounds mad, and he sounds a little jealous, too, when he complains that "You say my kisses are not like his." On this and other cuts on this album, Dylan's performance, his phrasing and timing and the good time he's having with the band, rescue this material from the brink of unbecoming self-indulgence. He may be mean and ornery and mad and tough and sad and regretful, but he's also with a bunch of good-old-boy musicians having a ball.

The love songs on Side One of the second record in this double album take up time, fill in the grooves. None are memorable. Dylan's voice sounds a little tired and hoarse on "Temporary Like Achilles"; there's some virtuoso harmonica playing on "Absolutely Sweet Marie." He laughs at himself a lot in "Fourth Time Around" as he describes a breakup once again from yet a different angle:

I stood there and hummed,
I tapped on her drum and asked her
how come . . . .
And gallantly handed her
My very last piece of gum.

But this is a transitional song, both about one breakup but also directed to someone else, someone new.

And when I was through
I filled up my shoe
And brought it to you
And you, you took me in,
You loved me then
You didn't waste time . . . .

Maybe that's why he can afford to be so glib and satirical, he's got something else going.

Just exactly what that "something else" might be is revealed in the epic love song that consumes the entire second side of the second record in this set: "Sad-Eyed Lady of the Lowlands." This song is a devout, adoring tribute to a new lady and a new relationship. Clearly this is the beginning of something quite momentous, so in awe of this creature does he seem. He describes her in terms that are both romantic ("your flesh like silk, and your face like glass") and mysterious, almost religious ("your saint-like face and your ghostlike soul")—while he himself assumes a very courtly, deferential posture:

Who among them would try to impress
you?
Sad-eyed lady of the lowlands,
Where the sad-eyed prophet says that
no man comes,
My warehouse eyes, my Arabian
drums,
Should I leave them by your gate,
Or, sad-eyed lady, should I wait?

Blonde on Blonde marks the apex of Dylan's career as a rock 'n' roll star. At this point in his life he really was as big as Elvis Presley. Moreover, the content of Dylan's songs convinces many idolatrous fans that he *knows*, that he has some cosmic *answer*, that he can tell them the truth about their lives—an assumption which he himself both encourages and disdains. "Listen to me," he says; but "Don't listen to me . . . ." The responsibility is too great, the pressure becomes immense.

It's amazing that amidst such confusion and while completing a frantic schedule of concerts and tours, he is able to write and record such a number of first-rate songs. For *Blonde on Blonde* is far more controlled than either *Bringing It All Back Home* or *Highway 61 Revisited.* It even expresses more effectively his preoccupation with the madness and absurdity of everything around him—his difficulty with women, the rage and anger and violence of his energy in the face of psychic assault. Musically, Dylan has reached a new level of mastery on *Blonde on Blonde.* Recording with these excellent country-rock musicians, he's produced primarily a group of love songs, each unique, each selected from his eclectic bag of styles, each appropriate to whatever part of his psyche he has chosen to express. And his playing and singing on these recordings are excellent.

> "Boy, I hurried . . . . I hurried for a long time. I'm sorry I did. All the time you're hurrying, you're not really as aware as you should be. You're trying to make things happen instead of just letting it happen. You follow me?—Bob Dylan"

In a *Rolling Stone* Interview © 1970 by Straight Arrow Publishers, Inc.

In this case the autobiographical facts are germane: years later, in the song "Sara" on the album *Desire,* we are told that Dylan "stayed up for days in the Chelsea Hotel writin' 'Sad-Eyed Lady of the Lowlands' for you . . ." Hindsight, therefore, reveals the importance of this song written as it was for the woman Dylan married. And you can hear that in this very moving performance: the sincerity, the precision of the singing as he hits a middle D and the low A on "Looowlands." It's a long song, yes; there are some who wish it were longer still.

Blonde on Blonde turned out to mark the end of a particularly busy period for Dylan, a time of tremendous growth and creativity and bewildering success. At that point, in 1966, it was impossible to predict where he would go from there.

Bob Dylan's Greatest Hits

Columbia Stereo KCS 9463 or Mono KKCL 2663. Released March 1967. Rainy Day Women #12 & 35, Blowin' in the Wind, The Times They Are A-Changin', It Ain't Me Babe, Like a Rolling Stone; Mr. Tambourine Man, Subterranean Homesick Blues, I Want You, Positively Fourth Street, Just Like a Woman. *All written by Bob Dylan.*

OPPOSITE: JIM MARSHALL REX FEATURES

ALLEGORIES, PARABLES

John Wesley Harding

Columbia KCS 9604. Produced by Bob Johnston. Released January 1968. John Wesley Harding, As I Went Out One Morning, I Dreamed I Saw St. Augustine, All Along the Watchtower, The Ballad of Frankie Lee and Judas Priest, Drifter's Escape; Dear Landlord, I Am a Lonesome Hobo, I Pity the Poor Immigrant, The Wicked Messenger, Down Along the Cove, I'll Be Your Baby Tonight. *All by Bob Dylan.*

John Wesley Harding marks the beginning of a new phase for Dylan, an important shift in direction, style, image, and attitude, a dramatic departure from the rock 'n' roll period of *Bringing It All Back Home, Highway 61*, and *Blonde on Blonde.* The Beatles have just released *Sgt. Pepper's Lonely Hearts Club Band,* and the Rolling Stones quickly follow that with *Their Satanic Majesties Request.* Dylan, therefore, chooses to make his dramatic reappearance *completely out of step.* While his rivals, doubters, and peers are moving further out, producing elaborate studio recordings with dubbings-over-dubbings accompanied by full symphony orchestras and wizard electronic gimmickries, Dylan produces a plain and simple acoustic record of unadorned, straightforward music. While others are exploding into the universe in search of the cosmic giggle, Dylan appears with his feet on the ground and the Bible in his hand. While everyone else was adding, he subtracted; they expanded, he contracted; as all around him seemed to increase, he decreased, concentrated, focused and produces not only a new musical synthesis but a hell of a lot to think about.

Dylan *could* have released an entirely different album. During his convalescence he had written many songs and made a lot of music which was later released on other albums or recorded by other artists, particularly The Band. But rather than let us hear that particular music at this time, Dylan chooses the music we hear on the finely honed, artfully pointed *John Wesley Harding.*

John Wesley Harding is a sermon disguised as a series of narrative ballads. The songs on this album are like gentle admonitions, sung in a mellow and persuasive voice. Like all of Dylan's music, there's a lot between the lines. There *is* a message. But instead of beating us over the head, Dylan herein assumes the mantle of a teacher, a rabbi, and a patriarch who shows the way through example, through moral allegory, and through parable. Each of the songs is short and to the point. Dylan takes a position. He has reappeared, liberated from the madness that had surrounded him. Apparently he is also free of those personal devils that had plagued him: anger, jealousy, bitterness. He reincarnates himself before our very eyes, regroups his energy, which had been faint, and carefully applies it to a new

Dylan's newest musical incarnation reflects both his own maturity *and* his keen sensitivity to public consciousness and taste. His new album consciously projects an abrupt change in identity from nearly burnt-out electric superstar to born-again family man — and he expresses this in a folk and country musical style which is in strong contrast to current hip trends. Dylan the pop star has been survived and succeeded by Dylan the patriarch, the teacher, the moralizing prophet, and the reasonable, loving man.

January 1968. Dylan makes a surprise appearance at Carnegie Hall during a memorial concert to Woody Guthrie. His first public performance since 1966, Dylan sings a few Guthrie standards, backed by The Band, then disappears again into the woods.

DAVID GAHR

Left: With Pete Seeger, Judy Collins and Arlo Guthrie at the Guthrie Memorial Concert

OPPOSITE: JIM MARSHALL

BOB DYLAN
JOHN WESLEY HARDING

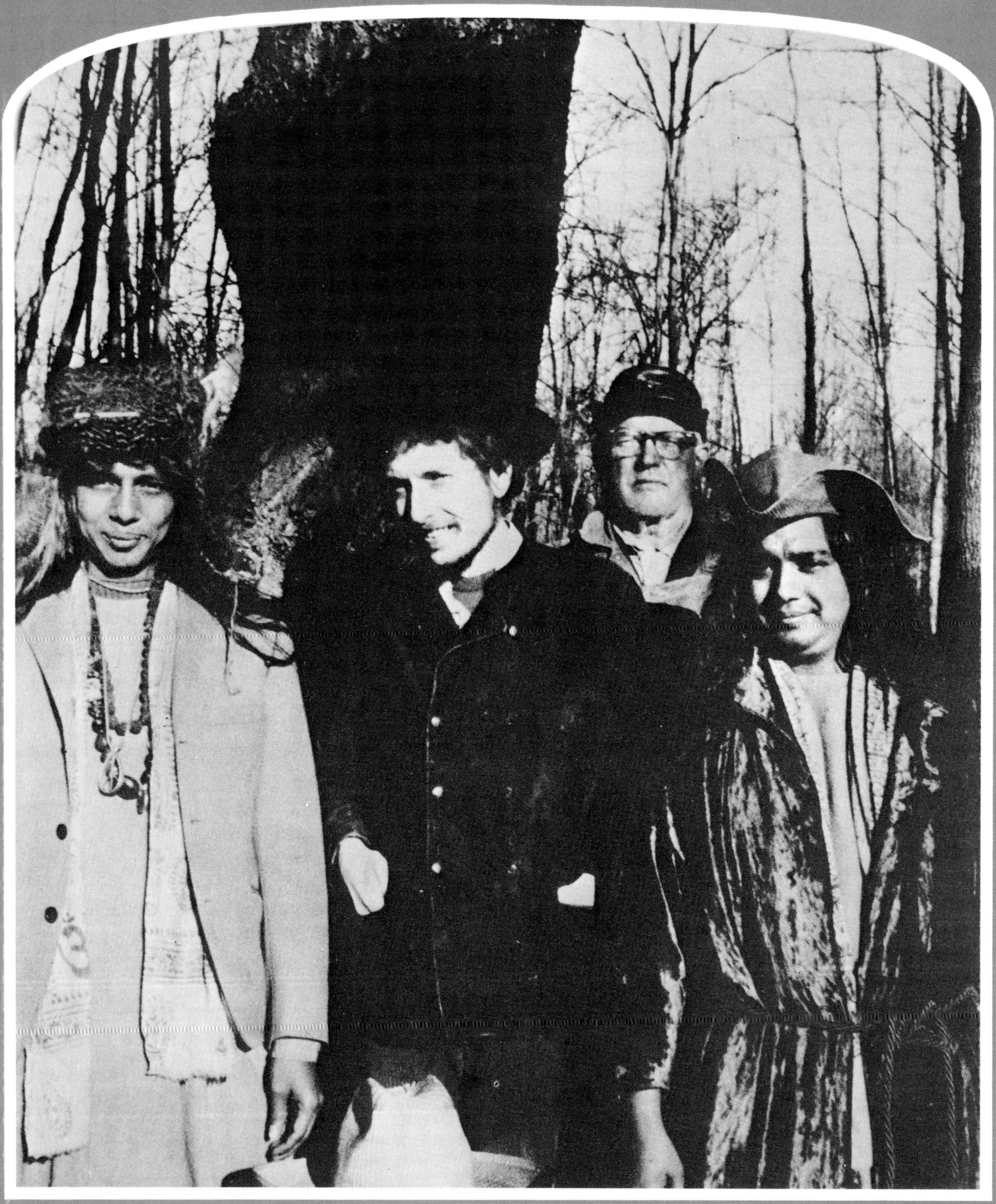

> "The long rest after the accident, the marriage to a young slim dark haired girl who resembles Joan Baez, the birth of two children, the tranquility of his country hideout in Woodstock, all have combined to produce a new gentler, more mature Dylan. The old tensions and angers seem gone forever." —Lillian Roxon
>
> The Sidney *Morning Herald,* 1968

> "The pressures were unbelievable. They were just things you could never understand because they did such weird things to my head."—Bob Dylan
>
> *Rolling Stone* © 1972 by Straight Arrow Publishers, Inc.

position. For all his protestation to the contrary, Dylan tells us once again: this is it!

And what is it? The *Bible*. Mostly Old Testament. And what does it say in the Bible? Well, there's the Ten Commandments, the Golden Rule, lots of advice about loving thy neighbor, striving for holiness and moderation. Dylan's previous moralizing had been so adolescent and simplistic, so good-versus-bad, us-versus-them. Now he's saying something much subtler: he's older and matured; he's learned something from all those years in the crucible; now he's saying in these cunningly plain, simple songs—with no electricity, with understatement rather than hyperbole—now he's advising us to love each other and take responsibility for our lives.

Dylan's deliberate image transplant with *John Wesley Harding* is apparent at first glance. The cover photo shows a candid, smiling, human-looking Dylan standing in a close group of Indians. Relaxed, unassuming, just hanging out in a black-and-white polaroid shot in the woods, out in the country. Just folks. Down home. And the first cut, the title song of this album, starts off with the sound of an acoustical guitar, just strumming away for a few bars, then Dylan's voice comes in: plain, earnest, a little tentative, and in a major key:

John Wesley Harding
Was a friend to the poor . . .

Wait a minute, was the cry across the country. Has Dylan gone back to his folksinger, Woody Guthrie days? Not really. He *is* reverting to the appropriate style for what he has to say, but this is no ordinary outlaw ballad; he's singing here about a special sort of fellow, a true Robin Hood who:

. . . was never known
To hurt a honest man.
. . . was always known
To lend a helping hand.
. . . was never known
To make a foolish move.

In short, an exemplary hero, *not* an angry or violent or judgmental hell raiser of a bandit but rather a virtuous man, a *moderate* man, an appropriate romantic model to represent this album and Dylan's new self-image.

"As I Went Out One Morning" is a curious, enigmatic parable wherein a woman in chains offers herself to him but he refuses.

I knew that very instant,
She meant to do me harm.

There's a bit of tugging and pulling, she tries her best to capture him but Tom Paine himself appears to take her away, apologizing:

"I'm sorry, sir," he said to me,
"I'm sorry for what she's done."

Curious, yes? Nearly harmed, almost seduced by a fair damsel, fighting her all the way and finally saved by the late, immortal revolutionary hero, free thinker and kindred spirit, Tom Paine. A more sophisticated, subtler song of revenge than, say, "Positively Fourth Street."

In "I Dreamed I Saw St. Augustine," still more virtuous heroes are recalled: the melody and opening words of this song are quite similar to the famous ballad "Joe Hill," written by Earl Robinson and Alfred Hayes. Remember Paul Robeson singing?

I dreamed I saw Joe Hill last night
Alive as you and me.
Says I "But, Joe, you're ten years
dead. . . . "
"I never died," says he . . . "I never
died," says he . . .

Dylan's frame of reference in this song is far greater than the union hero shot by the "copper bosses." Dylan is dreaming of a more exalted and mystical hero. He's out there with Saint Augustine himself, a man he probably finds it easy to identify with since Augustine was quite prey to the pleasures of the flesh before he became a pious and visionary philosopher/saint. More importantly, Dylan is deeply upset by his dream because *he* feels responsible for Augustine's death:

I dreamed I saw St. Augustine
Alive with fiery breath,
And I dreamed I was amongst the ones
That put him out to death.
Oh, I awoke in anger,
So alone and terrified,
I put my fingers against the glass
And bowed my head and cried.

What a moving and powerful image: Dylan appalled at his own behavior, repentant for however he might have caused this saint's death and all he stood for. Guilt. Repentance. Universal responsibility. And with it, he hopes, salvation.

"All Along the Watchtower" is only twelve lines long and takes two min-

> "Anyone who calls Dylan "the greatest poet in the United States today" has rocks in his head. That is such an irresponsible statement as to deserve no attention. Since his appeal (apparently) is to irresponsible teen-agers, I can't take him seriously. Dylan is for the birds—and the bird-brained."—English professor, University of Vermont
>
> Quoted in *The New York Times*

Spring 1968. **Dylan remains out of sight, enjoying more peace and quiet with his growing family. His father, Abraham, dies, and his second son is born. His relationship with Albert Grossman becomes more distant, and when their contract together expires a year later, it is not renewed.**

Fall 1968. **Dylan flies down to Nashville with only four new songs in his pocket to record a new album of country music. Quickly, he fills in the rest of the album on the spot, writing some songs in his motel room, some in the studio, and also cutting a few tracks with his old buddy Johnny Cash, who drops by during the sessions. The result is *Nashville Skyline*, an album which Dylan thinks is "the best record I've ever done."**

utes and thirty seconds to perform. Understated, precise, economical, this important song reveals still more of the overtly moral message Dylan is expounding throughout this album. It begins with a wonderful descending minor progression from A to B minor to G:

"There must be some way out of here," said the joker to the thief,
"There's too much confusion, I can't get no relief."

This joker sounds like the old Dylan, or Mick Jagger on "I can't get no satisfaction. . . ." But wait, this is only the premise, this joker is just a straw man:

"No reason to get excited," the thief, he kindly spoke,
"There are many here among us who feel that life is but a joke."

Dylan himself has been saying that for five years. But now he goes on to reject and transcend that childish point of view:

But you and I, we've been through that, and this is not our fate,
So let us not talk falsely now, the hour is getting late.

Dylan, brushed by death and blessed with rebirth, is telling us now to *avoid* the trap of existential angst, to eschew the irresponsible, cop-out attitude that life is just too crazy and meaningless for us to do anything about. No, he says, we've been through all that. Time is passing. Let's cut out the nonsense and get down to business. We're at the watchtower here, on the ramparts, there's no time for foolishness, life is *short.* Sure there's madness and confusion all around us; it isn't simple and it isn't easy. But it's up to *us* to make our own meaning. Life is no joke. *We* have to take charge of it, from within, for ourselves, warily, carefully, thoughtfully. No one's going to do it for us, either. Life's meaning and its rewards will come only from our determination, our hard work, high seriousness and—as we shall see—our love.

"The Ballad of Frankie Lee and Judas Priest" is a long story/song about two friends. Frankie needs money; Judas offers it quickly but Frankie's too proud to accept. Rather he covets the women in Judas' house and dies, foaming at the mouth, in the ravings of his insatiable lust. "The moral of this song," Dylan takes pains to tell us

Is simply that one should never be
Where one does not belong.

"In *John Wesley Harding* Dylan reiterates his belief that compassion is the only secular manifestation of the religious experience. . . . Indeed, while change in Dylan's universe is the natural state of things, impatience to implement change is the supreme form of egotism, the ultimate vanity: it is an individual's setting himself apart from the flow. Preoccupation with the methodology of change, like any magnification of one small aspect of the flow of life, implies a ceaseless intellectualization which precludes a possibility of the religious experience."
—Steve Goldberg

So when you see your neighbor carryin' somethin',
Help him with his load.
And don't go mistaking Paradise
For that home across the road.

Down with envy, away with all lust, and avoid, above all, the deadly sin of pride.

"Dear Landlord" is yet another remarkable homily. The landlord would appear to be a natural adversary, an enemy, the sort of bad guy Dylan opposed in the early days of "Masters of War." This gentle entreaty, however, advocates mutual understanding, compassion, and sympathy. Dylan sees it differently now. He can feel another man's suffering; he can empathize and identify with him in their common humanity:

I know you've suffered much,
But in this you are not so unique.
All of us, at times, we might work too hard
To have it too fast and too much.

This is a complex song musically, with fourteen different chords and a startling E7 change in the opening of each stanza ("Please don't put a price on my *soul.*"). It's a song of reconciliation, a far cry from his previous anger and simplistic vilification of anyone in a position of authority. More than a truce, it's a genuine offer of mutual respect, even friendship:

Now, each of us has his own special gift
And you know this was meant to be true,
And if you don't underestimate me,
I won't underestimate you.

In "I Am a Lonesome Hobo," Dylan is openly critical of his previous attitudes and, as in "My Back Pages," offers contrition for the mistakes of his past: for mistrust, greed, particularly his failure to accept responsibility:

. . . I did not trust my brother,
I carried him to blame . . . .

Each of us, he preaches, *must* take responsibility; there's no one else to take

"There were thousands and thousands of people just wanting that song ["Masters of War"], so I wrote it up. What I'm doing now isn't more difficult, but I no longer have the capacity to feed this force which is needing all these songs. I know the force exists but my insight has turned into something else. I might meet one person now, and the same thing can happen between that one person (and myself) that used to happen between thousands."
—Bob Dylan

From *Conversations with Bob Dylan* by John Cohen & Happy Traum. *Sing Out!,* October-November, 1968

> I'm tryin' to be like the medium at a seance. There's a mystery, magic, truth, and the Bible in great folk music. I can't hope to touch that, but I'm goin' to try. —Bob Dylan

To Michael Ischetta, 1967, op. cit.

the rap. And in closing he warns us against the things *he* used to do, admonishing us to follow a more righteous path:

But let me just warn you all,
before I do pass on;
Stay free from petty jealousies,
Live by no man's code,
And hold your judgment for yourself
Lest you wind up on this road.

"Judge not, lest ye be judged," as it says in the Bible. Lust not after false gods, either. This message is strongly reiterated in "I Pity the Poor Immigrant." Formerly this man did struggle and strive and wail and continuously fail, buffeted and disillusioned by life. Now he stands back from that desperate, futile quest with Olympian hauteur:

I pity the poor immigrant
Whose strength is spent in vain . . .
Who eats but is not satisfied,
Who hears but does not see . . .
Whose visions in the final end
Must shatter like the glass.

Vanity, vanity, all is vanity. Don't look elsewhere for the answer; don't expect to satiate your appetites or earthly desires. And there's a very curious line wherein he describes this poor fellow:

Who falls in love with wealth itself
And turns his back on me.

"Me" isn't capitalized or emphasized in any special way, but the implication seems to be that the immigrant has turned his back on something divine. Is Dylan playing God? It's only a song.

In "The Wicked Messenger," Dylan describes himself as the former proprietor of a mind "that multiplied the smallest matter." Dylan delivers this song in a cantorial, Jewish style, a Semitic whine that's consistent with the mideastern tone of the melody. Again, he admonishes his former self: "If ye cannot bring good news, then don't bring any," which is a remarkable thing for a songwriter to tell himself, particularly one who's been known to bring around a lot of bad news in his time.

Turning to *good news,* however, Dylan saves the last two songs on the album for a hint of what's been happening to him personally—on an otherwise impersonal album. These final songs reveal what it is that's been giving him such strength and calm and also what direction he'll be moving on to next, both musically and spiritually. "Down Along the Cove" is all about love, true love, love forever:

Down along the cove,
I spied my little bundle of joy.
She said, "Lord, have mercy, honey,
I'm so glad you're my boy!"

You said it. Dylan's voice is warmer, mellow, loving, sincere. But the best is yet to come. The climax of this album is the wonderful song "I'll Be Your Baby Tonight." It's as if he's saying, let me show you what it's really all about. I've told you how crummy it feels to be on your own; I've warned you not to blame everyone else; I've showed you how important it is to take charge, to assume responsibility for your own lives; I've also preached tenderness and love and compassion for your fellow humans . . . well, here's what it all comes back to: loving someone. *Really* loving. He's lucky. He's grateful. He's devoted. If ever a song seemed to be written by a truly happy man, it's this one. There's a gentle slide guitar in the background, lending a warm, languid feeling to the lovely chord changes, particularly the G major after the opening four bars of F. It's a very simple song, musically, with a sense of self mocking humor, as when Dylan speeds up on the lyric:

Well, that mockingbird's gonna sail
away,
We're gonna forget it.

Dylan's performance is so ingenuous we're convinced how happy he is. It's not that hard, he seems to be saying, just

Close your eyes, close the door,
You don't have to worry any more
I'll be your baby tonight.

It's a far cry from the messages and intentions of his previous incantations. How different he seems from the megavolted rocker of *Blonde on Blonde.* No more apocalyptic visions of despair to rationalize copping out or quitting life; no more frenzied search for meaning in hasty, enigmatic incident or transient relationships. He's centered, gathered his strength, and come home. He's feelin' confident, secure, independent, his own man. Almost thirty, he's reached a new level of maturity, as a father and a husband and a family man. He strongly advises us to follow suit. He's not shy, either, about telling us this is the way it's *supposed* to be. Had he been born a few hundred years ago, Dylan might very well have been a rabbi.

> What I've been doing mostly is seein' only a few close friends, readin' little 'bout the outside world, porin' over books by people you never heard of, thinkin' about where I'm goin', and why am I runnin', and am I mixed up too much, and what am I knowin' and what am I givin', and what am I takin'. And mainly what I've been doin' is workin' on gettin' better and makin' better music, which is what my life is all about.—Bob Dylan

In *Scarred Bob Dylan is Comin' Back* by Michael Ischetta, New York *News,* 1967

> In *Harding,* Dylan superimposed a vision of intellectual complexity onto the warm, inherent mysticism of Southern Mountain music, rather like certain French directors (especially Jean-Luc Godard) who have taken American gangster movies and added to them layers of 20th-century philosophy. The effect is not unlike Jean-Paul Sartre playing the five-string banjo. The folk element gains a Kafka-esque chimericality, and the philosophy a bedrock simplicity that leaves it all but invisible and thus easy to assimilate.—Paul Nelson

In *Rolling Stone* © 1969 by Straight Arrow Publishers, Inc.

Stereo
KCS 9825

Nashville Skyline

Columbia KCS 9825. Produced by Bob Johnston. Released April 1969. Girl from the North Country (*with Johnny Cash*), Nashville Skyline Rag, To Be Alone With You, I Threw It All Away, Peggy Day; Lay, Lady, Lay, One More Night, Tell Me That It Isn't True, Country Pie, Tonight I'll Be Staying Here With You. *All written by Bob Dylan.*

Do you *believe* the photograph on the front cover of this album? There's no title but the message is clear: beaming down at us with the filigree branches of a tree just framing his head against the clear blue sky, his one hand holding a beautiful, shiny guitar of inlaid wood, the other hand raised up as if to doff his good old hat. Aw, shucks! It's red-neck Bob Dylan in his first 101 percent, all-country album: *Nashville Skyline.*

Dylan had recorded in Nashville before: parts of *Blonde on Blonde,* all of *John Wesley Harding.* But this, his ninth album, is the first deliberate country-and-western recording, totally Nashville, both in style and intention. For whereas *John Wesley Harding* is a sermon—brilliant, understated, but didactic—*Nashville Skyline* is a *hoot,* a joyous celebration, a happy revelation. This has to be the happiest album Dylan has made till now: gentle, playful, calm, and serene. Everything about it conveys Dylan's new role of the family man, unperturbed, peaceful, patient, loving, and loved. What a difference between this country gentleman and the surly, angry, strung-out-looking guy on the front of his precrash albums *Highway 61* and *Blonde on Blonde.*

Dylan wants to tell us what's making him so happy, something he started to do on the last two cuts of *John Wesley Harding.* Let's count our blessings, he says, chief among which are our love and our loving families, the basic, mundane things in life—all the old eternal verities which country music has always been about.

Johnny Cash, the great country-and-western pop star, knows this. He, too, came back from a wild and reckless youth, saved by love. And Johnny Cash himself wrote the liner notes to this album: a kind of syrupy tribute to Dylan, corny but sincere, printed up there in the clouds over a back-cover shot of the actual Nashville skyline:

This man can rhyme the tick of time
The edge of pain, the what of sane. . . .
I'm proud to say that I know it,
Here-in is a hell of a poet.
And lots of other things
And lots of other things.

Johnny Cash also sings on the first cut of this album: "Girl from the North Country." It's a curious duet. Dylan sings his part in a very high tenor, much slower than the version on his second album, *Freewheelin'.* The two pals obviously hold each other in high esteem: their vocalizing is so respect-

Summer 1969. **Reaction to *Nashville Skyline* is extreme. On the one hand, angry critics complain he has sold out to the red-necks, he has gone commercial, he has produced an album of shallow muzak. On the other hand, some political theorists applaud him for another stunning revolutionary act: he has bridged the gap between the intelligentsia and the working class by writing truly blue-collar, proletariat music. Neither explanation is quite accurate – in fact, Dylan is doing what he's always done: writing from his experience, reflecting what is happening to him at the time, choosing to express, for now at least, a happy heart. His musical evolution is consistent with his early love of country and his long-standing ties to Nashville. He hasn't turned his back permanently on any of the musical styles in his repertory of identities, but rather added new vocal and musical possibilities with a characteristic eclecticism of style that best serves his state of mind.**

JIM MARSHALL

REX FEATURES

Dylan comes gradually out of seclusion. He makes several more surprise appearances at other people's concerts and recording sessions. He and his family move back to New York City to live in a Greenwich Village duplex near Dylan's former haunts.

In August, Dylan makes his first paid public performance in four years in England, at the climax of a two-day musical festival on the Isle of Wight. Two hundred thousand fans see a serene, subdued country gentleman dressed in a white suit singing some old songs like "Highway 61" and "Like a Rolling Stone" in a new, mellow voice. He's paid a reported $75,000 for singing one hour.

ful, they're constantly adjusting and making room for each other. Dylan tries thirds and fifths and tenths to Cash's melody line, touching occasionally a note that doesn't quite work but skittering away gracefully before it really sours. It's an artful, ingratiating improvisation. It also sounds like a rehearsal.

"Nashville Skyline Rag" is a rare Dylan number with *no words.* But does it *cook!* Dylan is at home in any camp; he bridges all cultural gaps. Heck, if he doesn't get down with these good old boys like Kenny Buttrey, Charlie McCoy, Pete Drake, and Charlie Daniels and do the country *boogie!* Musical sleuths have traced the origins of this rag to an unreleased Broadside recording called "The Cough Song" made way back in 1963. Evidently that guitar and harmonica version wasn't quite right, but Dylan kept that material in the back of his head for further full-flowering in this new version.

"Is it rolling, Bob . . . ?" Dylan asks his producer Bob Johnston at the opening of the third cut. His voice is resonant. Forget angst—this boy is having a wonderful time as he swings into his first real solo of the album, "To Be Alone with You." The feeling, the sentiment, and the words pick up right where "I'll Be Your Baby" left off:

To hold each other tight
The whole night through
Ev'rything is always right
When I'm alone with you.

"Love is all there is, it makes the world go 'round," he tells us on the next cut, somewhat ironically entitled "I Threw It All Away." This not-so-plantive ballad purports to be the sad story of a man who treated his lover "like a fool" and lost her to his everlasting regret:

You just won't be able to do without it.
Take a tip from one who's tried.

Well, he may have thrown love away and tried to do without it, but it's hard to believe he's suffering very much about it now.

Dylan's singing delivers a different message altogether: he doesn't sound miserable or brokenhearted at all. It's a country-and-western tradition to deliver melancholy songs with a straight face or at least a long-suffering stiff upper lip. Dylan goes beyond this, delivering this instructional tale from a storyteller's or teacher's distance, as if to say: you see, children, this is what could happen to you like it once happened to me, albeit a long time ago. *Now,* of course, it's a different story,

> In *Nashville Skyline* . . . Dylan is surrendering the surrogate joys of genius for the emotional joys of the maturity which genius must pursue in vain. . . . Alone, *Nashville Skyline* is a tightly written, cleverly executed series of cliches that would seem to be merely a collection of nice songs written by a Dylan who has gotten a bit mentally plump. As the final step in Dylan's search for God, however, it is a lovely paean, Dylan's acknowledgment of the joy of a life suffused with compassion and God.
> —Steven Goldberg

WIDE WORLD PHOTOS

now I've found—as he goes on to sing on the next cut—"Peggy Day."

There are about eleven major chords and changes in "Peggy Day." The number really swings. In this single performance, Dylan's vocal style ranges from Fats Waller to Al Jolson to a show-biz, Las Vegas Elvis Presley whammo at the finale. Jesus, no wonder this album drove some former fans up the wall, it's such a departure. This boy could play the borscht circuit in the Catskills, the lounge at Caesar's Palace, or the Grand Ol' Opry itself. Listen to this word play in "Peggy Day":

Peggy night makes my future look so
bright,
Man, that girl is out of sight,
Love to spend the day with Peggy
night.

The next cut, "Lay, Lady, Lay," has become something of a standard, frequently aired on middle-of-the-road easy-listening stations. Dylan wrote it originally for the film *Midnight Cowboy,* but they used Fred Neil's song instead. It's a mellifluous, languid love song, which can appeal to just about every human being on the face of the earth. The very sound of all those repeated *I*'s sooths our troubled brows. It's all so simple, Dylan says over and over on this album: turn off the light, be alone with your lover, and love, love, love, all through the night. The message in this song may be as important as any Dylan has ever preached before:

Why wait any longer for the world to
begin
You can have your cake and eat it too
Why wait any longer for the one you
love
When he's standing in front of you.

The instrumental backing on this song

is brilliant: the electric slide guitar, the percussion, the slight echo in the vocal engineering.

"One More Night" is another quick take on lost love, again with no real despair or unhappiness in the performance. Oh, yes, he may be "as lonesome as can be," but this time he refers to his former love as "the only pal I had." No bitterness or anger here . . . sounds like he'll get her back all right, and everything's going to be just fine.

"Tell Me That It Isn't True" sounds a lot like "All I Really Want to Do" from the *Another Side of Bob Dylan* album way back then, particularly at the line "All I would like you to do . . ." But whereas the older song is a whine, a harangue, a defiant plea for at least a stand-off, this new song *could* convince a woman that she should change her mind. It's not threatening, it's downright persuasive.

All of those awful things that I have
heard,
I don't want to believe them, all I
want is your word.
So darlin', I'm countin' on you,
Tell me that it isn't true.

"Country Pie" is a delightful musical hoedown, celebrating the joys of good music and good eating in a razzmatazzle musical potpourri that sounds like the children's songs Woody Guthrie used to write so endearingly (i.e., "Jiggle-jiggle-jiggle-jiggle, tickle-tickle-tickle-tickle, little sacka sugar I could eat you up!"). Dylan doesn't usually write songs exclusively for children, but there's something about this number that comes from being a father and living with kids. It'd be hard for a man who didn't live with kids to write a lyric like:

Raspberry, strawberry, lemon and
lime
What do I care?
Blueberry, apple, cherry, pumpkin
and plum
Call me for dinner, honey, I'll be
there.

There's more to this than singing and eating, though, as Dylan slips in some more about-face philosophizing:

I don't need much and that ain't no lie
Ain't runnin' any race
Give to me my country pie
I won't throw it up in anybody's face.

"Tonight I'll Be Staying Here with You" concludes this album with a restatement of the theme first expounded in "I'll Be Your Baby Tonight" and repeated throughout "To Be Alone with You," "Peggy Day," and "Lay, Lady, Lay." All of these love songs are the opposite of his old songs of bitterness and breaking up and running off. He's not threatening to leave in these songs, nossir, he's positively intent on *staying:*

Throw my ticket out the window,
Throw my suitcase out there, too,
Throw my troubles out the door,
I don't need them any more
'Cause tonight I'll be staying here with
you.

Nashville Skyline is a delightful album—fun to listen to, fun to work out and play yourself on the piano or guitar, fun to sing along with. The songs on this record constitute a new kind of Declaration of Dependence, in complete contrast to the defiant independence he'd fought for since "Restless Farewell" and *The Times They Are A-Changing.* Now Dylan has turned his back on those "troubles." He's at peace with himself, and the music shows it.

RETNA

"Searching out the sources of every sort of American music—from the rock and roll childhood he shares with his fans to the depression ballads our parents might have known, from the apocalypse of Robert Johnson to the city flash of Muddy Waters, from the old testament of the Carter Family to the ageless earth of Johnny Cash—Dylan found what he was looking for, and his impact on the Sixties has been devastating and magnificent. And that impact is perhaps as much a result of Dylan's personal stance as it is a result of his music. Hard to find, hard to find out about, Dylan held back from the usual nonsense and the honest curiosity that surrounds the star and created, perhaps to protect himself, perhaps for fun, a style of resistance, allegory, irony and humor that pervaded both his songs and his appearances in public.—Greil Marcus"

In *Rolling Stone* © 1969 by Straight Arrow Publishers, Inc.

REX FEATURES

Dylan appears to be casting about. People want to follow him, but they aren't sure where he's leading, or if they still trust him after so many radical shifts in direction.

Moreover, he chooses this moment to release a bizarre, controversial double album of pop standards and songs, many of them written by other people, called *Self-Portrait*.

Self-Portrait

Columbia C2X 30050. Produced by Bob Johnston. Released June 1970. All the Tired Horses (*B. Dylan*), Alberta #1 (*B. Dylan*), I Forgot More Than You'll Ever Know (*C. A. Null*), Days of 49 (*F. Warner, J. A. Lomax, A. Lomax*), Early Mornin' Rain (*G. Lightfoot*), In Search of Little Sadie (*B. Dylan*); Let It Be Me (*M. Curtis, P. Delance, G. Becaud*), Little Sadie (*B. Dylan*), Woogie Boogie (*B. Dylan*), Belle Isle (*B. Dylan*), Living the Blues (*B. Dylan*), Like A Rolling Stone (*B. Dylan*); Copper Kettle (*The Pale Moonlight*) (*A. F. Beddoe*), Gotta Travel On (*P. Clayton, L. Ehrlich, D. Lazar, T. Six*), Blue Moon (*L. Hart, R. Rodgers*), The Boxer (*P. Simon*), The Mighty Quinn (Quinn the Eskimo) (*B. Dylan*), Take Me As I Am (Or Let Me Go) (*B. Bryant*); Take A Message to Mary (*F. Bryant, B. Bryant*), It Hurts Me Too (*B. Dylan*), Minstrel Boy (B. *Dylan*), She Belongs To Me (*B. Dylan*), Wigwam (*B. Dylan*), Alberta #2 (*B. Dylan*).

On the front of this *Self-Portrait* album is a self-portrait, a painting of Bob Dylan by Bob Dylan. Dylan is a painter. He's been painting and drawing for years, mostly in a very spare and simple style something like the illustrations Woody Guthrie did for his autobiography *Bound for Glory.* (You can see a good sampling of Dylan's drawings in the book *Writings and Drawings by Bob Dylan,* Knopf, 1973.) This front-cover self-portrait, however, seems to be an oil painting, kind of primitive and childlike, done with broad, deliberately crude strokes: big nose, ears sticking out, small mouth, heavy brows, short hair, not very pretty. Is this how Dylan sees himself? Not very flattering.

The album *Self-Portrait* isn't altogether flattering either. There's some good music, an interesting oddity or two, but it's a very mischievous album. Despite the title, there's not much new or original material on the album; rather Dylan has chosen to sing things written by other people and also to include some live recordings of his own work in versions that are quite different from what we've heard before. Two records. Twenty-four songs, including some standard pop songs

COLUMBIA RECORDS

***June 1970.* Dylan is awarded an Honorary Doctorate of Music from Princeton University and surprises many by showing up at the ceremony to receive his degree in person. The enigma continues to mystify and confuse.**

WIDE WORLD PHOTOS

***June 1970* (*continued*). *Self Portrait* provokes widespread hostility among critics and fans. Dylan is accused of deliberately alienating his constituency, of selling his soul to commercial demands, of destroying his talent and losing his creative integrity. Ralph J. Gleason, one of Dylan's greatest admirers and the acknowledged dean of rock writers, is so offended he calls for a Bob Dylan boycott. Public empathy and popularity for Dylan reaches a new all-time low.**

Above: With Walter Lippman at Princeton

***October 1970.* Dylan claims not to be perturbed, in fact he's defiant. He defends *Self-Portrait* with pride and predicts history will vindicate his explorations and experiments and new directions.**

you'd never have expected him to record, like "Let It Be Me" and "Blue Moon."

Dylan calls this album *Self-Portrait.* Why? Because it does present him in many disparate incarnations: the crooner, the country star, the old folkie, the laid-back rocker, the whiner and wheezer. There's a variety of vocal and musical styles jumbled together on this recording, which was produced with the help of a long list of personnel listed on the inside cover: David Bromberg, Ken Buttrey, Charlie Daniels, Rick Danko, Levon Helm, Garth Hudson, Doug Kershaw, Al Kooper, Charlie McCoy, Richard Manuel, Robbie Robertson, Maeretha Stewart, and a host of others.

There's a loose sort of foolin' around feeling on *Self-Portrait,* with some odd little fillips thrown in, as if to say: I'm all these things; *this* is me and *this* is me and, wait a second, *this* is me, too. Dylan feels good. He's asking for a little self-indulgence, a chance to relax after all these years, just for himself. He wants to be outrageous. And outrage *was* the general reaction to this album at the time. *It drove people right up the wall.*

Some former Dylan freaks never recovered from the first cut: "All the Tired Horses." Dylan himself doesn't sing in this song, rather there's an angelic women's choir, some pretty high sopranos repeating the line:

All the tired horses in the sun,
How'm I s'posed to get any ridin'
done. . . .

. . . then humming forever: "hmmmm-mmmmmmmmmm . . ." just humming like all get out. It's kind of sweet. Maybe it's existential or has a lot of symbolic meaning ("Horses," they always stand for something; and "Riding" does sound a lot like "writing"). Maybe it's a takeoff on an old Roy Rogers movie. Can you blame people

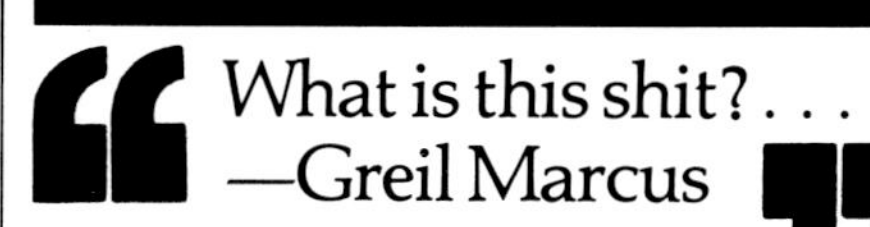

In *Rolling Stone* © 1970 by Straight Arrow Publishers, Inc.

for being mystified?

Self-Portrait goes on from this bizarre opening to all sorts of other surprises: "Alberta #1" is a slooow and laaazy number with what sounds like some dynamite black lady singers vocalizing in the rear. It's called "#1" because there's another version of the same song, "Alberta #2," on the last cut of Side Four of this album—a faster, tighter, and whiter version than #1. In "I Forgot More Than You'll Ever Know," Dylan croons a beautiful country classic in his Elvis Presley voice. In "Days of '49" he reverts to an older, folksy style for this long ballad of the Gold Rush, originally collected by the folklorist Lomax family. "Early Mornin' Rain," a song by Gordon Lightfoot, provides Dylan the opportunity to assume one of his favorite poses: the Spanish/Mexican/Latin lover. And in "In Search of Little Sadie" he attempts a Doug Kershaw impression: Cajun, with weird, playful chord changes, pace changes, vocal gyrations. They may have called this "In Search Of" because they truly got a little lost. This cut sounds like a rehearsal for the second version which appears only two bands later and is much more together. But why has Dylan included both takes? Only The Shadow knows the answer to these and other mysterious questions. For example, did Bob Zimmerman stand outside the senior prom with his nose pressed to the window and is that why he's chosen to take his revenge with his very formal, two-step, high-school-dance version of "Let It Be Me"? We'll never know.

> It's certainly a rather odd "self-portrait": other people's songs and the songs of a few years ago. If the title is serious, Dylan no longer cares much about making music and would just as soon define himself on someone else's terms. There is a curious move toward self-effacement; Dylan removing himself from a position from which he is asked to exercise power in the arena. . . . —Greil Marcus

In *Rolling Stone,* © 1970 by Straight Arrow Publishers, Inc.

One begins to feel like a Jewish scholar, searching for hidden meaning in every ink spot, every accidental comma of the Bible. Why, for example, is the music for "Woogie-Boogie," a cooking, nonvocal instrumental number, included in Dylan's official songbook whereas the twice-recorded "Little Sadie" isn't? Dylan, incidentally, is notorious for recording a song in one single take. In this instance, however, he seems to be insulting us with a rehearsal cut of "Sadie" before we get to hear the second, far more polished version. And why does Dylan use violins and an orchestral background for what could have been a simple, beautifully sung ballad, "Belle Isle," and is it significant that this, too, is left out of the musical canon though, like "Sadie," it's attributed to Dylan? And why, for that matter, didn't he do another take on "Belle Isle" since he must have realized his singing is slightly off-key at several points. Could this be part of his self-revelatory, self-portrait process? Is this how he shows us how imperfect he can be? Yes, I'm no leader and I'm no superman either; it's just plain human being me. Could be . . .

"Living the Blues" is an unqualified success, a hard, good-time rock 'n' roller that sounds a lot like the old Guy Mitchell song "Singing the Blues." Dylan gets down, he's really into it with the highest energy yet demonstrated on this album. The female back-up group is swell, too. Why wasn't this a big hit single? But just to keep us off-balance, the next cut is a live recording of "Like a Rolling Stone" as performed at the Isle of Wight concert with The Band. The vocal is nothing like the original, hard-bitin' version we've known and loved these many years. This time Dylan pours out the words in a torrent, a continuous, slurred-together blur. Nevertheless, this surprising, unorthodox version of the old classic is powerful, largely through the interaction of Dylan's soaring vocal against the driving, big-beat wall of sound from The Band. And when Dylan shouts out the words "Just like a Rolling Stone," the crowd goes wild!

"Copper Kettle" is a sleepy, boozy song about making moonshine, sort of an instructional guide. Dylan sounds half-asleep or drunk himself, assuming the role of the old distiller hunkering down around his gear in the middle of the woods. It's one of the best performances on the record. What an actor! "Gotta Travel On" has

> "The power of those recordings [*Bringing It All Back Home, Highway 61 Revisited, Blonde on Blonde,* "Like a Rolling Stone" and "Subterranean Homesick Blues"] and of the music Dylan was making on stage, together with his retreat at the height of his career, made Dylan into a legend and virtually changed his name into a noun. Out of that Dylan gained the freedom to step back and get away with anything he chose to do, commercially and artistically. . . . In a real way, Dylan is trading on the treasure of myth, fame and awe he gathered in '65 and '66. In mythical terms, he doesn't have to do good, because he has done good. One wonders, in mythical terms of course, how long he can get away with it.—Greil Marcus"

some fine licks on the guitar and a tambourine that breaks up the beat into a million shimmering pieces. "Blue Moon" caused more consternation than any other cut. Many took it as the most awful of Dylan's idiosyncratic digressions. It's a formal, mournful version of the old pop standard with a beautifully sad violin solo accompaniment that trails off in a tragic coda at the end like a sad, cantorial Fiddler on the Roof.

"The Boxer" is a song by Paul Simon. In this curious version, Dylan sings both the Simon and the Garfunkel parts, overdubbing himself with two voices, one smooth and mellow, the other hoarse Dylan voice from the early sixties. It almost works, but unhappily the two tracks are not always together, either harmonically or rhythmically. One more take might have done it! Similarly "The Mighty Quinn" has the sound of a homemade recording. Somewhere through the muddy engineering, though, you can hear Dylan and The Band really whooping it up with this rousing song with the infectious refrain:

Come all without, come all within
You'll not see nothing like the mighty
Quinn.

Dylan didn't write "Take Me As I Am," but the song has an obvious message: this is me, folks, with my guard down, my back turned, my defenses put aside. Listen to the piano and violin on this cut. "Message to Mary" could have been better if the tracks had been remixed with a better balance. As it is, Dylan's vocal is nearly overpowered by the instrumental backing. You can hardly hear him—he sounds so faint and far away. Why did they release this uncorrected? In sharp contrast is the beautifully balanced "It Hurts Me Too," my own favorite song on the record. Dylan repeats a theme here that he first presented in "All I Really Want to Do" (on *Another Side of Bob Dylan*): I don't want to be your boss, I just want to be your man (and again on "Tell Me That It Isn't True," from *Nashville Skyline*). In fact this version is more convincing, so appealing is the vocal. Dylan's tight, dramatic vibrato on "*Looove,* you baby" is thrilling.

> "The point is that Dylan's songs can serve as metaphors, enriching our lives, giving us random insight into the myths we carry and the present we live, intensifying what we've known and leading us toward what we never looked for, while at the same time enforcing an emotional strength upon those perceptions by the power of the music that moves with his words.—*Rolling Stone*"

"Minstrel Boy" features a duet between Dylan and Robbie Robertson that is positively pious. You can just see them standing together in long white robes at the front of a fundamentalist Baptist church. It's beautiful, it's religious, it's truly harmonious, what fine and dignified vocalizing. "She Belongs to Me" is another live performance from the Isle of Wight, a rushed, sort of offhand version of the venomous old song first released on *Bringing It All Back Home.* "Wigwam" is hypnotic, an instrumental, Latin sound, with Dylan Dadaing and lalaing against some punchy horns and a good drum. It's like riding horseback down a sandy, dirty trail over a few rolling hills and then up on a ridge overlooking the plain where the tepee is nestled in the distance: home. *Soporific!* You'd think it was the end of the album, but no, there's one last cut, "Alberta #2," tighter, faster than "#1" and featuring a great harmonica duet with a piano in constant syncopation.

So *Self-Portrait* does have some interesting stuff among the mischievous quirks and sloppy throwaways and off-the-wall inclusions. But why are we so apologetic? Maybe because Dylan was crucified at the time. Because people were quick to jump on him and write him off as finished, through, washed up, soldout, dullsville. How fickle, how absurd, how shallow. They just weren't listening carefully, as Dylan himself pointed out at the time. And how eager they were to close in for the kill. As the dust settled and years passed, *Self-Portrait* has become more appreciated for what it is: experimental, self-indulgent, foolin' around, with peculiar lapses but odd flashes of brilliance and innovation.

Just to cover his bets, however, Dylan goes back to Nashville and quickly records a new, completely different album which is released only four months after *Self-Portrait.* This new album is nothing like that controversial double album: the songs are original, the music has tremendous vitality, the entire recording is infused with love and exaltation and is appropriately entitled *New Morning.*

RENEWED MORNING

BOB JENKINS   OPPOSITE: REX FEATURES

New Morning

Columbia KC 30290. Produced by Bob Johnston. Released October 1970. If Not For You, Day of the Locusts, Time Passes Slowly, Went to See the Gypsy, Winterlude, If Dogs Run Free; New Morning, Sign on the Window, One More Weekend, The Man in Me, Three Angels, Father of Night. *All by Bob Dylan.*

New Morning seems to have been produced with unprecedented haste. Perhaps the howls of critical protest over *Self-Portrait did* have some effect. Does Dylan want to show us he can still knock us out, like Muhammad Ali, loafing through one fight, then coming back to stun us with the next? In any event, *New Morning* is clearly a very major effort, one of the very best albums Dylan has ever produced and a stunning popular and artistic success.

Just look at that face on the cover. How earnest, how manly. It's one of the best-looking, most intimate, open faces Dylan has ever allowed us to see. No more poses or abstractions, this is a level-headed portrait of the artist having survived chaos and come out the other side. Serious. Focused. He seems to be saying: "Now pay attention, people, it's me again, I'm back here in full power, and I've got something to tell ya."

Turn over the album for another surprise: Young Bobby Zimmerman, chubby-cheeked, scruffy-clothed, shyly peeking out at the camera, standing there next to the great Victoria Spivey in a photograph taken at the historic Big Joe Williams session. A young boy, just starting out, holding a guitar next to the beaming black

November 1970. *New Morning* does restore Dylan to popular and critical esteem. Ralph J. Gleason hails the album ecstatically in a column headlined: "We've Got Dylan Back Again." Dylan has proved himself again. He's come out swinging, and the verdict is unanimous — he's still the greatest!

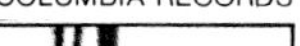
COLUMBIA RECORDS

FRED W. McDARRAH

May 24, 1971. **Dylan visits Israel for his thirtieth birthday and prays at the ancient, holy Wailing Wall in Jerusalem. He has visited Israel with his family several times as his sense of Jewish identity increases over the years. He sends his children to a religious Jewish summer camp and considers a one-year residence at an Israeli kibbutz, Neve Eitan. When his application is delayed, however, he hesitates and moves on. . . .**

WIDE WORLD PHOTOS

woman at the piano. There's a point to this, of course—it reminds us of where he's come from and also indicates something about this recording, which has a lot of black feeling to it and a hell of a lot of good piano playing, too, both by Dylan and by Al Kooper.

The album begins with a love song: to his wife, to us, to the muse? Whomever . . . It's called "If Not for You," and the point is he can't get along without it:

Without your love I'd be nowhere at all,
I'd be lost if not for you
And you know it's true.

Similar in style and intention to the sequence of love songs on the *Nashville Skyline* album, Dylan performs this song with determination and high energy. We can tell right away there's going to be no fooling around on this album.

"Day of the Locusts," a title reminiscent of the Hollywood novel by Nathanael West, is actually about Dylan's accepting his honorary degree from Princeton University. We usually associate locusts with the plague, but in this case Dylan uses them as a kind of Greek chorus representing God and nature, chirping away, "singing for me," as the academy confers upon him its approval. Dylan has accepted this degree with ambivalence, with mixed feelings. Mrs. Martin Luther King and Walter Lippman also received honorary degrees on that muggy New Jersey afternoon, which he vividly describes:

DAVID GAHR

The man standin' next to me, his
head was exploding,
Well, I was prayin' the pieces wouldn't
fall on me.
Yeah, the locusts sang off in the
distance,
Yeah, the locusts sang such a sweet
melody.

You can actually hear the locusts at the opening of the song, there's some tough piano playing throughout the cut, and the story ends with his high-tailing it out of there with his sweetheart back to the hills and the woods and the places all the locusts hang out. It was weird, Dylan seems to say, and he feels more comfortable with the applause of nature than the bouquets of ceremonious men.

DAVID GAHR

The dynamite piano playing continues on "Time Passes Slowly." This child is *good.* He's got *rhythm,* and he's been practicing, too. There are eleven chords in this lovely song and that's a lot. There's a message, too:

Ain't no reason to go up, ain't no
reason to go down,
Ain't no reason to go anywhere.

Just hold still, he says and be like "the red rose of summer." . . .

. . . that blooms in the day
Time passes slowly and fades away.

Safe there, out in the woods at last, Dylan stays put. Stands pat. Good advice and nice work if you can get it.

"Went to See the Gypsy" is a delightful put-down of all the muddy-headed true believers who've ever

> "Salvation means many things in Dylan's songs. On one level it is the conquest of guilt, ambition, impatience, and all the other obsessive states of egotistic confusion in which we set ourselves apart from the natural flow of things. On another it is the supremely free flight of the will. On still another it is faith, an acceptance of a transcendent, omnipresent godhead without which we are lost. —Steven Goldberg"

been seduced or taken in by a false guru. In this narrative, Dylan, in the role of the Moonie-Jesusfreak-Baba-daber is told by a pretty dancing girl to:

Go on back to see the gypsy,
He can move you from the rear,
Drive you from your fear,
Bring you through the mirror,
He did it in Las Vegas,
And he can do it here.

Las Vegas! Is that a testimonial? Is that a *warning*! Sure enough when he goes back, the holy fellow is gone: run off with the dancing girl. Flesh wins out again, folks, as the number ends with some musical cooking, a regular blast of tightly played hot music, just to set all this lewdicrosity in the proper perspective.

"Winterlude" is music to ice-skate to. It sparkles like a portrait from Grandma Moses, with snow and ice and a cozy log fire to lie near with your loved one. It's a waltz—lilting and lazy—which Dylan sings to his lover endearingly and with tremendous affection:

Winterlude, Winterlude, my little apple,
Winterlude by the corn in the field,
Winterlude, let's go down to the chapel,
Then come back and cook up a meal.

What fun! How loving! And he ends it all with the genuine sentiment: "Winterlude, this dude thinks you're grand."

The last cut on the first side is the funky bluesy "If Dogs Run Free." Yes, all this good stuff, and we're still on Side One. This number is a set theatrical piece, a terrific job of acting, a little play, in fact, which Dylan recites over Al Kooper's boogie-woogie piano and the virtuoso scat singing of background vocalist Maeretha Stewart. We can see him there sitting at his table in the pool hall, putting on the mantle of a black street philosopher:

If dogs run free, then why not we
Across the swooping plain?. . .
True love needs no company,
It can cure the soul, it can make it whole,
If dogs run free.

Truer words were never spoken. There are *fifteen* chords in this song, and everyone is playing like a *fiend.*

The second side of this album opens with the title song, "New Morning," and a bang-up opening for the second act it is, too: a wonderfully positive, upbeat song with such a splendid

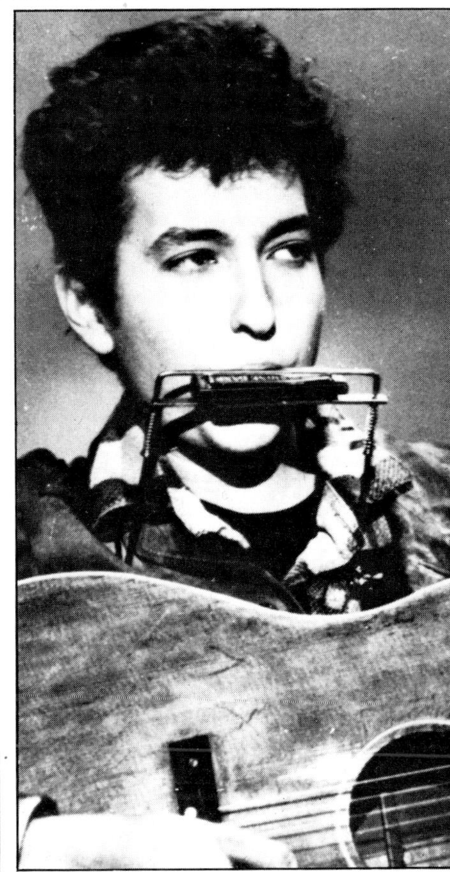
WIDE WORLD PHOTOS

WIDE WORLD PHOTOS

WIDE WORLD PHOTOS

"Dylan is . . . a man who has been through many of the changes we have been through ourselves, and is still going through them; the difference is that, unlike most of us, he has been able to write songs about what has been happening to him all the way along.—Craig McGregor"

Introduction to *Bob Dylan: A Retrospective,* © 1972 by Craig McGregor

FRED W. McDARRAH

August 1, 1971. **Dylan makes a surprise appearance at George Harrison's benefit concert for Bangladesh. A packed house at Madison Square Garden is thrilled to see Dylan give a brilliant performance of several old protest songs from the 1960's — including "Blowin' in the Wind" — all sung in one of his old voices. This dramatic flashback causes some to hope that Dylan will return to politics. In any case, Harrison's check for $243,418.50 in box office receipts from Madison Square Garden is sent to the United Nations Children Fund for relief to Bangladesh.**

Below: With George Harrison and Leon Russell at the Concert for Bangladesh

infusion of loving energy in the rub-a-dub beat, the inventive guitar playing, the exalted spirituality of the words, and the infectious high energy of Dylan's singing. It's inspirational. Listen to how he opens with "Can't you hear that *rrooooster* crowin'?" There are fourteen or so chords in this deceptively complex song, with a neat progression from A to C#/G3 to A/G to Fm to D, that lifts us right off our feet, ready to join Dylan and follow him anywhere:

So happy just to be alive
Underneath the sky of blue
On this new morning, new morning
On this new morning with you.

"With *you,*" he sings, "with *you.*" With his wife, his children, his friends, even *us*. Dylan sings this uplifting anthem like a man reborn, or like an orthodox Jew praising the Lord every morning as he wakes, for the universe, for life, for love . . . amen and count your blessings.

"Sign on the Window" is a carefully wrought melodrama, which Dylan sings in a precise, theatrical style, like a miniature play. It's the story of a man whose woman runs off to California with another boyfriend. Ominous signs confront our hero: "Lonely . . . Y'don't own me . . . . Three's a crowd." And she's gone. Dylan muses on the possibility of continuing rain as the key changes from minor to major, and our narrator determines to make a new start:

Build me a cabin in Utah,
Marry me a wife, catch rainbow trout
Have a bunch of kids who call me "Pa."

Sounds good. Sounds like what Dylan has done. But the last two lines of the song have a touch of irony about them, even doubt, both in the writing and in the performance:

That must be what it's all about,
That must be what it's all about.

He sounds a little worried, as if he knows it's not quite that simple.

"One More Morning" is a black-and-blue love song with Al Kooper on the piano. What a lot of *good* piano playing there is on this album. In the spirit of "New Morning," Dylan here celebrates the joys of being alone with his love. In this instance he's persuading her to abandon domestic chores. Yes, everything will be all right if they can just get away alone together—the classic cry of the husband to the long-suffering mother/housewife:

Things will be okay
You wait and see.
We'll go someplace unknown,
Leave all the children home,
Honey, why not go alone
Just you and me.

Has she been complaining? The man is out making a living while the woman waits at home. Sound familiar?

"The Man in Me" opens with a rapturously happy Dylan lalaing all over the place with that "Lay, Lady, Lay" use of the mellifluous l's. He's happy, and he's grateful:

Storm clouds are raging all around
my door,
I think to myself I might not take
it any more.
Take a woman like your kind
To find the man in me.

Couldn't be clearer than that. Dylan's willing to tell us now, without any symbol or deception or hidden, double-data meaning:

The man in me will hide sometimes to
keep from bein' seen,
But that's just because he doesn't
want to turn into some machine.
Took a woman like you
To get through to the man in me.

So many of these songs are written to this woman; his wife, his lover, and the mother of his children.

The last two songs on the album ac-

> It's confusing to me to think of how I reached whatever place this is. I tend not to wonder about it anyway. It's true, I have no goal so to speak . . . [except] to make the work interesting enough in order to keep doing it . . . . My intention would be not to think about it, not to speak about it, or remember any of it that might tend to block it up somehow.
> — Bob Dylan

From *Conversations with Bob Dylan* by John Cohen and Happy Traum, *Sing Out!* 1968

JOSEPH SIA

centuate the religious tone that has permeated this album. The first, "Three Angels," is delivered in a spoken, schmaltzy style something like an O. Henry tale of Christmas lost. Dylan's watching three angels on a city street, but no one else has noticed them. Are they cardboard cutouts? Are they just leftover decorations? Or are they *real* angels down from heaven, and everybody's just too busy to notice, too swept up in the vanities of earthly business to see them or hear their music:

The angels play on their horns all day,
The whole earth in progression seems
to pass by.
But does anyone hear the music they
play,
Does anyone even try?

Dylan sees and Dylan hears. And he's not putting the others down, as he might have before, but wondering when, O Lord, when they'll look up and see the light. . . .

Dylan has saved the best for last. "Father of Night" concludes this album with a prayer: the kind of prayer you might say with your children, holding hands around the dinner table or at bedtime before they all go off to sleep—a prayer of thanks and celebration, a reverential, pious prayer to the omnipotent, to God, to the power beyond ours, the power that creates day and night, mountains and clouds, cold, heat, grain, wheat, who makes time and gives us dreams, a prayer of praise to the unknowable, all-encompassing Father of Life.

Father of air and Father of trees,
Who dwells in our hearts and our
memories,
Father of minutes, Father of days,
Father of whom we most solemnly
praise.

"Father of Night" is short and to the point. It's one of the best prayers you'll ever hear anywhere—a lesson in the economy of plain speaking.

So the champ bounces up off the floor and delivers a knockout punch. The doubting Thomases crucified him for *Self-Portrait*—seen in historical perspective as a kind of busman's holiday. But Dylan quickly returns to deliver a new album full of light and love, tight energetic songs and some terrific piano playing. Not just romantic songs idealizing this love, but rather showing us how he's working out the snags and doubts and anxieties. Complexity, variety, clear-thinking, direct-saying, virtuoso musicality—the new, improved, renewed, risen again *New Morning.*

> This album is a sign. You believe that? I think I do. It is surely the best thing new to come over the airwaves and out of the grooves in I don't know when and after these grim weeks of Agnew and Reagan and Nixon and Billy Graham and all that shit, it was like the cool, clear water from a mountain spring to hear his voice so true, so good. . . . —Ralph J. Gleason.

In *Rolling Stone,* © 1970 by Straight Arrow Publishers, Inc.

FRED W. McDARRAH

> I never said "Don't expose me" in *New Morning,* what's that?
> *Backwards, backwards, you know you play a part of it backwards.*
> And it says "Don't expose me?"
> *Yeah.*
> Oh, *fuck,* man *Jesus.* . . . Why don't you play an Andy *Williams* record backwards, if you . . ."
> —Bob Dylan

To Alan J. Weberman, *Rolling Stone,* © 1971 by Straight Arrow Publishers, Inc.

***October 1971.* Dylan chases and physically attacks one A. J. Weberman. For several years, Weberman has accused Dylan of being a heroin addict and has actually been stealing the Dylan *household garbage* to filter through for clues. After trying to cooperate and befriend him, Dylan negotiates a promise from Weberman to desist. When Weberman breaks this agreement, Dylan allegedly tries assault and battery.**

***November 1971.* Dylan is restless. He plans a one-hour TV special for Christmas, but it never comes off. He tries out some new music with Leon Russell but doesn't produce enough satisfactory stuff for an entire album.**

78

He records and quickly releases a single, "George Jackson," a bona-fide "protest" song about the murder of this famous Black Panther leader in San Quentin prison. But then rather than produce a new recording of entirely fresh material, he puts out an album of old hits plus six "new" songs—some from way back—which have never before been released.

Bob Dylan's Greatest Hits, Volume II

Columbia KG 31120. Released November 1971. Watching the River Flow, Don't Think Twice, It's All Right, Lay, Lady, Lay, Stuck Inside of Mobile with the Memphis Blues Again; I'll Be Your Baby Tonight, All I Really Want to Do, My Back Pages, Maggie's Farm, Tonight I'll Be Staying Here with You; She Belongs to Me, All Along the Watchtower, The Mighty Quinn (Quinn, the Eskimo), Just Like Tom Thumb's Blues, A Hard Rain's A-Gonna Fall; If Not for You, Baby Blue, Tomorrow Is a Long Time, When I Paint My Masterpiece, I Shall Be Released, You Ain't Goin' Nowhere, Down in the Flood. *All by Bob Dylan.*

In contrast to other compilations, including his own first volume of *Greatest Hits,* Dylan has produced six "new" songs for this *Volume II* album that had never before been released, including some very interesting material from three distinct periods of his work: 1963, 1967, and the time of this release, 1971.

The first, "Tomorrow Is a Long Time," goes way back to a live performance in 1963, the period of *Freewheelin' Bob Dylan.* Quiet, sad, accompanied on his acoustic guitar, the young Dylan sings this forlorn song of romantic love in a simple lyrical style:

Yes, and only if my own true love was waitin',
Yes, and if I could hear her heart a-softly poundin',
Only if she was lyin' by me,
Then I'd lie in my bed once again.

Eight years ago, then in his early twenties, Dylan pines for an idealized love of Suze Rotolo that had not, in fact, been fully realized. Contrast this sense of loneliness and frustration with the cycle of loving, confident, mature songs recorded from *John Wesley Harding,* through *Nashville Skyline* and *New Morning.* The change is evident: Dylan eventually found what he was looking for. But in this early, plaintive song he expresses the loneliness and yearning of his younger self.

Three songs from this album were recorded in 1971 but were written in 1967, during the period Dylan spent in Woodstock recuperating from his motorcycle accident. So why weren't they released on *John Wesley Harding?* Well, in fact, Dylan wrote a lot of music during this period that he didn't record or release himself, some of which other artists like The Band did release, some of which came out on pirated bootleg recordings like the famous *Basement Tapes,* and some of which he did release or rerecord, as on this double album. The point being, Dylan didn't want to diffuse the specific statement intended by the album *John Wesley Harding* with material that didn't fit, either stylistically or in terms of the content, the message he was trying to put out after that long silence.

In any case, he has finally presented us with three gems from that period in 1967, here recorded with the help of Happy Traum on bass, banjo, second guitar, and vocal harmony. The first, "I Shall Be Released," was made famous by The Band in a slower, more theatrical version. On this cut, Dylan swings into the song with a positive upbeat delivery, giving more emphasis perhaps to the double level of meaning working throughout. The singer's in jail, behind walls, the man next to him claims he was framed, he's hoping for release. But the singer's also all of us, down here on earth, each of us with our little spark of the divine, our light shining within, waiting to be released and reunified with some greater power, some ultimate rejoining with the divine.

I see my light come shining
From the west unto the east.
Any day now, any day now,
I shall be released.

The power of this song is downright religious. It's an expression of Dylan's own expectation of immortality, his own hope of unification, of rejoining with some kind of godhead. It's about that salvation that Jewish mystics describe when they say each of us is like a fragment of the great fire that will someday be regathered and renewed. Dylan wants to get off, to break out, to be free. The "release" could be the release of death, but it feels more like the fervent hope of universal transcendence.

"You Ain't Goin' Nowhere" is performed—again with the help of Happy Traum—in a style of vocalizing

> "Who *ees* he? inquired Zsa Zsa.
> "He's the most famous rock star in the world!" said Huntington Hartford, speaking quickly.
> "Oh, *vell* then," said the Zsa, brightening. "I *luhv* him!"
> Dylan approached, put his arm around Zsa Zsa, and the photo was snapped. "Be sure to send me a copy," he reminded the *Newsweek* lady.—Timothy Ferris

quite reminiscent of The Band. Their work together and influence upon each other has clearly been great. This is a joyous, happy song about settling down in the anticipation of marriage:

Whoo-ee! Ride me high
Tomorrow's the day
My bride's gonna come
Oh, oh, are we gonna fly
Down in the easy chair!

The third and final song in this sequence, "Down in the Flood," also sounds a lot like The Band in its vocal style: the plaintive, high, close harmony of Dylan and Traum sounds like the way Richard Manuel, Rick Danko, Robertson, and Helm sing together.

Finally, this album includes two songs recently produced by Leon Russell, each with that distinctive Russell sound: a rocking, piano, harmonica, funky blues guitar, a big beat with sudden dramatic changes. It sounds like Little Richard is playing with Muddy Waters. "Watching the River Flow" opens with the surprising, ironic lines:

What's the matter with me,
I don't have much to say.

Dylan claims to be quite detached from all the angst and confusion around him, all those things that used to bother him so much:

People disagreeing on all just about
everything, yeah,
Makes you stop and all wonder why.
Why only yesterday I saw somebody
on the street
Who just couldn't help but cry.

The song has a kind of easy rhythm and happiness to it that seems to say, "Hey, cool it, don't let the world hassle or upset you too much." But it's a temporary pose; we know Dylan's got *a lot* to say. After all, he's saying this, he's singing us this song. We sense this is a very temporary hiatus, a brief vacation:

Wish I was back in the city
Instead of this old bank of sand . . .
But right now I'll just sit here so
contentedly
And watch the river flow.

The second new song is similar in its intention. Again, Dylan portrays himself as the semireluctant artist. No I can't always hack it, I'm not always going to do what you want or what's expected of me. In "When I Paint My Masterpiece," he's really making fun of all those expectations of genius that, well, maybe he'll never get around to. In this playful, irreverent song he describes himself glibly bopping around the world, in Rome, in Brussels, where all the masterpieces come from, the capitals of European culture, just an American kid who's never going to be like that, however he may aspire, mocking himself about how

Someday, everything is gonna be
diff'rent
When I paint my masterpiece.

Of course, you could say that Dylan's already produced quite a few masterpieces. But the pressure to top himself is constant, and in this protest he cleverly deflates both our expectations and his own.

So there you have it: a Christmas gift package: a collection of great old songs, an interesting sampling of previously unreleased material, an interim album to titillate our desire for more, more . . . .

The Concert for Bangladesh

Apple STCX 3385. Produced by George Harrison and Phil Spector. Released January 1972. Side Five: A Hard Rain's Gonna Fall, It Takes a Lot to Laugh/It Takes a Train to Cry, Blowin' in the Wind, Mr. Tambourine Man, Just Like a Woman. *All by Bob Dylan.*

JOSEPH SIA

January 1972. **The now legendary Concert for Bangladesh is released in a three-record set, which includes Bob Dylan's five songs, plus performances by George Harrison, Ringo Starr, Leon Russell, Billy Preston, Ravi Shankar, and others. The recording rises to the top of the charts and wins several awards as best album of the year.**

Later, 1972. **Still moving restlessly from project to project and place to place, Dylan falls into a chance to pursue his lifelong lust to make movies. His pal Rudy Wurlitzer sends him the script he's written for the Hollywood film *Pat Garrett & Billy the Kid.* They need a title song, so Dylan cuts a demo, which is keenly appreciated by the film's superstar director Sam Peckinpah. Peckinpah asks Dylan to write all the music for the movie soundtrack *and* to act in a major role.**

BOB JENKINS

Pat Garrett & Billy the Kid

Columbia PC 32460. Produced by Gordon Carroll. Released 1973. Main Title Theme (Billy), Cantina Theme (Workin' for the Law), Billy 1, Bunkhouse Theme, River Theme; Turkey Chase, Knockin' on Heaven's Door, Final Theme, Billy 4, Billy 7. *All written by Bob Dylan.*

Bob Dylan has had a continuous flirtation with the film business. He's wanted to be in the movies, but he's been smart enough to know that the vehicle, the property, the people he'd be working with—the overall creative and artistic control—had to be just right for his unique personality and abilities. When Albert Grossman was his manager back in the early 1960's, a few tentative efforts were made to option film properties that might have been suitable for Dylan's cinematic debut, but nothing ever came of this. In 1966, the Pennybaker group made a fascinating documentary film of Dylan's tour of England called *Don't Look Back.* And Dylan appeared in another small film, *Eat the Document,* which also had limited distribution.

Always on the lookout, Dylan accepted an offer from some friends and colleagues to work on the film *Pat Garrett & Billy the Kid.* He saw it as a chance to learn about the art of cinema, to see how movies are really made and to observe first hand the byzantine, inside-machinations and politics of the Hollywood film business. The experience was an education in how—with even the best intentions and the good efforts of some firstclass professionals—a movie can become a dismal disappointment.

This multimillion-dollar Hollywood production starred James Coburn, Kris Kristofferson, Jason Robards, and some other fine actors like Katy Jurado, Chill Wills, and Slim Pickens. Most importantly it was directed by the legendary Sam Peckinpah, who'd won both commercial and intellectual applause for such films as *The Wild Bunch* and *The Getaway.* Rudy Wurlitzer, an important young American novelist (*Nog, Quake,* and the screenplay for *Two-Lane Blacktop*) had written the screenplay. Moreover, Dylan was signed on not only to write and perform the soundtrack music, but also to act in what was alleged to have been a major role: that of "Alias," friend to

BOB JENKINS

> "And then we had to rope these damn *turkeys.* I couldn't believe it but Bob did it all. I couldn't *believe* it. I've seen prints and he's got a presence on him like *Charlie Chaplin.* He's like a wild card that none of 'em knew they had. I think they just hired him for the name and all of a sudden you see him on screen and all eyes are on him. There's something about him that's magnetic. He doesn't even have to move. He's a *natural.* —Kris Kristofferson"
>
> *Rolling Stone,* © 1973 by Straight Arrow Publishers, Inc.

Dylan resolves to use this opportunity as a learning experience; he wants to make his own movie someday. He and his family pack up for Durango, Mexico, where the film is being shot with Kris Kristofferson, James Coburn, Jason Robards, Rita Coolidge, and Katy Jurado. Dylan plays the role of Billy's sidekick throughout the long process of shooting — and also writes all the film's background music. The original soundtrack recording is produced both in Los Angeles and at the CBS Discos studio in Mexico City. Booker T. Washington (of Booker T. and the MG's), Roger McGuinn (of the Byrds), Russ Kunkel, Bruce Langhorn, and others play with Dylan on this abortive recording, which mirrors the confusion and mixed results of Peckinpah's ill-fated film.

November 5, 1973. **Dylan goes into the Village Recorder's Studio B in West Los Angeles with The Band to produce a major new album. By November 9, they're finished.**

Meanwhile reaction to both the film and the music for *Pat Garrett & Billy the Kid* is less than enthusiastic. Why did he do it? people ask, and what went wrong? It's been nearly three years since Dylan's last full-fledged album, *New Morning.* What's he doing and when will the rumored new album finally appear?

Above: With Kris Kristofferson and Rita Coolidge

BOB JENKINS

"Rudy needed a song for the script. I wasn't doing anything. Rudy sent the script, and I read it and liked it and we got together and he needed a title song. . . . So I wrote that song real quick and played it for Sam and he really liked it and asked me to be in the movie. I want now to *make* movies. I've never been this close to movies before. I'll make a hell of a movie after this.—Bob Dylan"

hero Billy, an enigmatic sidekick, a sort of wise fool who knows all, a kind of one-man transcendental Greek chorus and ultimate messenger of the film's cosmic meaning.

Things didn't turn out exactly as planned. Strange rumblings occurred during the film's shooting. Peckinpah was rumored to be way behind schedule and way, way over budget. Peckinpah made changes in the script, particularly in the part of "Alias." Peckinpah had conflicts with Dylan himself—or so the story goes. Later, the film was discovered to run far too long, and the studio made huge cuts without Peckinpah's approval. The original intention of the film was not realized, and one of the chief victims of the failure was clearly Dylan. Nearly all of his part seems to have wound up on the cutting-room floor. What remains of "Alias" is enigmatic to the point of meaninglessness—he's inscrutable to the point of absurdity. And as a result of pruning the film down to convenient length, the entire movie suffers from disjointed cutting and great gaps in continuity.

Nevertheless, the soundtrack album for *Pat Garrett* does include a little interesting music. It's reminiscent of the score Vincent Lopez wrote for a film called *The Fighter,* starring Richard Conte, way back in the fifties and also shot in Texas and Mexico. There's a lot of horseback riding music and saloon music and bunkhouse music—all in a very easygoing, occasionally dramatic Latin/Mexican style that Dylan has used before with some success. There are some really fine musicians playing with Dylan on this album, including Booker T. (of the MG's) Washington, Roger McGuinn, Bruce Langhorn and Russ Kunkel. Official production credit is given to the film's producer, Gordon Carroll, and the album has a rich, multilevel, many-track Hollywood sort of sound to it.

There are three separate versions of the title song ("Billy 1," "Billy 4," and "Billy 7"). Each has a different flavor, arrangement, and tempo. My favorite is "Billy 4," which was recorded in Mexico City. Dylan's vocal is strongest on this take, particularly in the verse wherein he advises Billy regarding women:

Hang on to your woman if you got one
Remember in El Paso, once, you shot one
She may have been a whore, but she was a hot one

Billy you been runnin' for so long.

One senses that Dylan's attitude toward this particular outlaw is not quite like his veneration of, say, John Wesley Harding. "Billy 1" and "Billy 7" are slower, darker, lower, and nearly drowned in a murky echo chamber.

"Turkey Chase" features some wizard Scruggs picking on the banjo by Jolly Roger, whoever that is. It's an evocative, finger-snapping, foot-stomping number. Like a lot of the music on this album, it has the energy of some action it was meant to be heard behind. "Knockin' on Heaven's Door" is a slow, ponderous, gloomy song, which perfectly depicts the movie's sense of Billy's impending doom:

Mama, put my guns in the ground
I can't shoot them any more
That long black cloud is comin' down
I feel like I'm knockin' on heaven's
door. . . .

Doom and death. Hopeless circumstance and dismal fate. Pointless murder and betrayal—it captures the flavor of the film.

This *is,* we mustn't forget, movie music: made-to-order, contrived to fit the action on the screen, often to provide specific mood and emphasis mood. Movie music is tailored by the director (and his editor) to fulfill their dramatic needs. Dylan, therefore, has done an exemplary job of providing music for Peckinpah's vision: dirge-like, dark, ominous, fatalistic. It's made-to-order music, and as such Dylan has done a professional job. It's *not* the most distinguished music or musical performance that Dylan has delivered. It must be reckoned as one of his lesser efforts and certainly the one over which he has exercised the least control.

BOB JENKINS

"The original soundtrack of *Pat Garrett & Billy the Kid* is an extension of its myth-destroying predecessor *Self-Portrait,* a record which further eliminates the possibility of anyone placing Bob Dylan on a pedestal. It is every bit as inept, amateurish and embarrassing as the earlier album . . . .

It is ironic that the most significant white rock figure of the Sixties has turned himself into one of the least significant of the Seventies. But the most perplexing aspect of it all seems to be the deliberate intent behind the decline. I can think of no other way to explain the gap between the man's earlier accomplishments and the recent dissipation of the quality of his work. But whatever the explanation . . . Bob Dylan has once again broken the mold, only this time, with the least acceptable method available to him, an album neither exceptional, nor truly different, but merely awful.—Jon Landau"

In *Rolling Stone,* © 1973 by Straight Arrow Publishers, Inc.

As if to muddy the water further, Dylan engages in a contractual dispute over the renewal of his agreement with Columbia, with which he's recorded since the beginning of his career. When negotiations break down, Dylan surprises everybody by signing with Elektra/Asylum. It's announced that Dylan has committed himself to doing two records for Elektra/Asylum: first that long-awaited big album; then a live recording to be made during a series of concerts planned for a gala national tour with The Band.

Consequently Columbia Records—perhaps in retaliation, perhaps in a fit of pique—also releases a bizarre album of old outtakes called *Dylan.*

DYLAN
Spanish Is The Loving Tongue
Mary Ann

Dylan

Columbia PC 32747. Produced by Bob Johnston. Released 1973. Lily of the West (*E. Davies, J. Peterson*), Can't Help Falling in Love (*G. Weiss, H. Peretti, L. Creatore,*), Sarah Jane, The Ballad of Ira Hayes (*P. LaFarge*); Mr. Bojangles (*J. J. Walker*), Mary Ann, Big Yellow Taxi (*J. Mitchell*), A Fool Such As I (*B. Trader*), Spanish Is the Loving Tongue.

This album is an unintentional aberration. It is *not* a record that Bob Dylan meant to be produced or packaged or released as such. Rather it's a kind of corporate bootleg, a collection of old rejects and outtakes released unilaterally by Columbia Records during a period of conflict and dispute between the parties which culminated in Dylan's signing with Elektra/Asylum and leaving, temporarily, the company he had been recording with since his first album in 1962.

Consequently everything about this album is peculiar and suspect. Entitled simply *Dylan,* the album reveals little about Dylan or what he was doing at the time. Adorned with a mysterious "Front cover serigraph," the art diffuses and disguises Dylan's face, distorting it through a silk-screen and stencil design process, which effectively obscures any real sense of Dylan's presence—objectifying and hiding him from our view. Moreover, most of the songs on this record are written by other people, having been recorded but not considered worthy of release during the *Self-Portrait* period. Two are listed as being in the public domain, and the one song, "Sarah Jane" has no credit. The song might have been written by Dylan, but if so, it has not even achieved the worthiness in Dylan's eyes of being included in his official songbook.

It's difficult to comment upon such an unauthorized batch of irregular, unplanned, and uneven material. Nevertheless there's something to be said for parts of this record. "Lily of the West" could have been a lovely ballad, but the vocal is overwhelmed by the accompaniment, the tracks are unbalanced, and the whole thing sounds like a rehearsal. "Can't Help Falling in Love" again features a somewhat tentative vocal from Dylan, accompanied by an organ, Elvis Presley style. One more take might have done it. "Sarah Jane," the only "original" song on the album, features a women's chorus joining Dylan for a whole bunch of "lalalaing." It's a very happy song about how wonderful it is to have a wife and five children—rushed through and not entirely convincing in this rendition. Would that we could hear another.

"The Ballad of Ira Hayes" is a powerful song, one of the best on this album. Written by the late Peter LaFarge, it's the sad but true story of a great war hero, an American Indian with no money, no crops, no chance . . . who dies Drunken Ira Hayes. Dylan's performance is one of the best and most replayed versions of this tragic ballad. Another fine cut is "Mr. Bojangles," a classic by Jerry Jeff Walker that Dylan himself could have written. Dylan sounds a little hoarse in this recording, but his rendition is as fine as any we've heard. "Mary Ann" is credited to the public domain. It's easy to forget the moment it's over, as I did both times. "Big Yellow Taxi" is a potentially funny song about how "you never know what you got until it's gone." Paradise is paved over to make parking lots, and trees are relegated to a museum. The arrangement, with its high-pitched female chorus in the background, sounds as if it was prepared for Petula Clarke, but the words and music might very well have worked in a different style and setting. In other instances, with other songs, Dylan has done another take in a radically different arrangement. This time he evidently didn't have the chance . . . or the desire.

"A Fool Such as I" is the best cut on the album, a cooking version of the good old ballad, with a hot group of Nashville cats really wailing behind his terrific vocal. Everyone gets off, the energy is high, Dylan is focused, it's a first-class production. "Spanish Is a Loving Tongue" has some nice singing. It's good to hear Dylan working on his Spanish in this Mexican persona, crooning like crazy in front of a chorus of gay senoritas.

JASPER DAILEY

That's all. No liner notes, no information about the actual recording dates, no credits or lists of personnel. The packaging seems cursory, almost vindictive in its throwaway obscurity.

This is an album of Dylan but not *by* Dylan. There's some interesting stuff but also a lot of material Dylan would likely *not* have allowed out if he had been in control.

***January 1974.* The bowdlerized *Dylan* album from Columbia has been preceded by *Pat Garrett* and *Greatest Hits Volume II.* There has been no major Dylan album since *New Morning*—four years ago. Passion for the mythic hero has been stifled and frustrated; his power and reputation reach an all-time low. Some critics literally write Dylan off as a feeble has-been. Others say that he has deliberately cut himself down from legendary to human size in some perverse weakness of character or selfish desperation to survive.**

FRED W. McDARRAH

OPPOSITE: CHUCK PULIN

TORCH BALLADS, CAST-IRON SONGS

CHUCK PULIN

PLANET WAVES
MOONGLOW
CAST-IRON SONGS & TORCH BALLADS

Planet Waves

Asylum Records 7E-1003.
On a Night Like This, Going Going Gone, Tough Mama, Hazel, Something There Is About You, Forever Young; Forever Young, Dirge, You Angel You, Never Say Goodbye, Wedding Song. *All written by Bob Dylan.*

Hindsight reveals Dylan's cycles, the ups and downs, the bursts of energy with fallow periods in-between. He rose like a flaming meteor from 1961-1966; then his motorcycle crash precipitated a necessary pause, a lying back and regrouping, which was followed by another rush of creativity from 1968-1970, the years which included *John Wesley Harding, Nashville Skyline,* and *New Morning.* Next came a relatively unproductive period, so far as publicly released material was concerned, e.g., *Greatest Hits Volume II, Pat Garrett & Billy the Kid,* and the unauthorized *Dylan.*

Planet Waves marks the beginning of a new cycle. It's a powerful, ambitious album, by far his best since *New Morning.* The entire project radiates high energy, tremendous intensity, and deliberate intent. Dylan wants to tell us something, and he's back to doing everything himself, just to make sure we get the message. These songs are *Planet Waves;* they're emanations from far within the earth, from the center: great washes and tides, powerful forces from deep inside of us and our world. As it says on the front of the album, these songs are cast-iron songs, sturdy, solid, permanent, tough, and well-built. And they're torch ballads of love—love with a fire, flaming passions, hot and sultry and burning. Yes, he tells us all this in stark black and white on the album's front-cover art, painting another self-portrait, too, with heavy serious eyes and a mouth set with purpose. But he portrays himself this time in a group, with a friendly, supportive back-up head on either side. Out of the center of his forehead, where a third eye might have been, grows an anchor. And on his right side, his heart itself appears, pierced by an arrow. Mark this well, fellow iconographers: an *anchor,* his heart *pierced by an arrow,* those heavy Jewish eyes, with the

MICHAEL ZAGARIS

***January 1974.* Once again, Dylan proves this negative speculation with a burst of tremendous activity and fruitful creative energy. In January he embarks on an historical national tour with The Band, his first in eight years and most ambitious ever. The tour plays nearly forty shows in twenty-five major cities across the United States and Canada. Hundreds of thousands of people spend somewhere between $4 and $5 million for tickets to see Dylan sing from his entire repertoire of old and new material. Dylan delivers a series of intense performances — enthralling rapturous audiences in the nation's largest arenas and concert halls — from the Oakland Coliseum to Madison Square Garden. The pop star sings to his audience like a rabbi, entertaining them with familiar stories, teaching them with moral homilies, exposing his heart in a new series of very personal songs. The virtuoso performs a tour de force, generating a tremendous amount of publicity, impressing one and all with his sustained and undiminished charisma, his brilliance as a performer, the growth of his ever-changing persona, and the spirituality of his new, more intimate compositions.**

Concurrent with the tour, the major new album entitled *Planet Waves,* which he had recorded in Los Angeles the previous fall, is released.

Spring 1974. Planet Waves restores Dylan to both critical acclaim and popular success. For the first time in his career, Dylan has a record at the top of the best-selling album charts for three weeks in a row. Moreover, the album is quickly certified "gold" (meaning sales of over $1 million) by the Recording Industry Association of America.

FRED W. McDARRAH

legend "Moonglow" traced on the sleeve of his arm.

This homemade, hand-done packaging for this record is loaded with symbols and signals, forecasts and outright proclamations of high seriousness and great purpose. On the back, Dylan has in his own hand written the credits for The Band, the engineer Rob Fraboni, and his assistant Nat Jeffery. He's thanked Robbie Robertson for "Special Assistance" but it's obvious that there's been no official producer other than Dylan himself. He's done it all. And in case we miss the point, he's written album notes to make it perfectly clear that he's starting out again, that this recording is another new beginning, an evaluation and consolidation, a gathering of all that has come before and a great leap forward:

Back to the starting point! The kickoff, Hebrew Letters on the wall . . . Bong—I dropped a double brandy and tried to recall the events . . . .

Dylan thanks his lucky stars, amazed at all that has come so far and eager, thrilled to be plunging ahead. He sums all this up in only 250 words, with mystic frames of reference and Eastern Old Testament flavor, wrapping up the madness and confusion, the lovers and strangers ("Yeah the old days are gone forever, and the new ones ain't far behind, the laughter is fading away . . . ."). Now he embraces his "brothers of the flood" and is jubilant that:

From there, it was straight up—a little jolt of Mexico, and some good LUCK, a little power over the Grave, some more brandy and the teeth of a lion and a compass.

We can sense him focusing and ready to fly—the very first cut, "On a Night like This," starts out with a big bang! On one level, it's an invitation to us all: let's get together and COOK! But it's also one of those torch ballads he promised us, a very hot, sexy love song, welcoming a woman that he's known and loved real well, urging her to come to bed and get it on. In the spirit of "I'll Be Your Baby Tonight," "To Be Alone with You," and "Tonight I'll Be Staying Here with You," Dylan herein celebrates a man ready to be swept away sexually by a good friend, partner, lover, wife. But in contrast to those gentler songs, this number is so stark, so powerful, Dylan just bites and hisses and spits and punches out the words with an animal ferocity:

"The Jewish people began their history as a tribe of wanderers who evolved into spiritual, as well as physical, nomads. The rabbis teach us: on Mount Sinai, Moses not only saw the letters of Torah, but also heard the silence (the hidden meanings) between the letters. The Talmud further teaches: when Moses descended from Mount Sinai and saw the people prostrate before the Golden Calf, he shattered the first set of Tablets, the first letters and silences of Torah.

Bob Dylan is one of a succession of Jewish mystics—Yitzhak Luria, Avraham ben Samuel Abulafia, Moses Cordovero, Rav Avraham Yitzhak Kuk, Rav Schneur Zalman, Rav Arele Roth, Rav Nachman of Bratzlav, and others of blessed memory—who have searched for, and tried to reintegrate, that fractured original vision: rediscovering the silences, and "raising the sparks" contained within each soul "to the fire." Poets are given gifts of understanding, teaches one rabbinic sage in the Zohar, denied even to angels . . . .

Bob Dylan is a post-Holocaust Jewish voice, searching for and rediscovering the manifestations of God. He has told me: "I have never forgotten my roots. I am a Jew.""
—Stephen Pickering

In *Bob Dylan Approximately: A Portrait of the Jewish Poet in Search of God,* © 1975 by Stephen Pickering

FRED W. McDARRAH

On a night like this
So glad you came around
Hold on to me so tight
And heat up some coffee grounds . . .
Run *your fingers down my spine*
Bring me a touch of bliss . . .
And let it burn, *burn,* burn, *burn*
On a night like this.

It's sexy as hell; it's the mature passion of a man for a woman he's loved; it's an act of seduction itself with its powerful sensuality and open desire; yes, and these folks have been together for quite some time now:

Put your body next to mine and Keep me company . . .
If I'm not too far off I think we did this once before.

He sings this ironically, humorously, playfully. And you can feel the blood rising; you bet they're going to have a wonderful time together. This is one of the funkiest, rankest, hottest sex songs Dylan has ever written. And it's sung in a tense, insistent style, pushing The Band's big beat, *not* that tender but *hard,* not all that soft but downright bestial, not all that sensitive but damn pushy, as if to say cut the shit and let's get down. Yes, there is a bit of impatience and a sort of steamroller quality here, as if there's some resistance to overcome.

One thing for sure: the love songs on this album are aptly called "torch" ballads. Dylan does seem to be *burning* with fierce love on *Planet Waves.* Burning isn't always fun, either. It can hurt. Such a consuming fire can be a mixed blessing, combining great pleasure with intense pain.

The next cut, "Going Going Gone," seems to be a breakout song, an updated "Restless Farewell." A grim Dylan appears to be busting out of tethers, throwing off the restraints that had bound him and anxious to be free again:

I been hangin' on threads
I been playin' it straight
Now, I've just got to cut loose
Before it gets late
So I'm going, I'm going, I'm gone.

There's an ominous Dm chord on that word "gone" which conveys a sense of danger and transition and dark, dark brooding. Is he itching for escape from some love that chains him? Or is he fed up with life itself, just running away to avoid self-destruction:

I been walkin' the road
I been livin' on the edge
Now I've just got to go
Before I get to the ledge . . . .

"The compression of story is masterful, but its real wonder is in the spaces, in what the artist left out of his painting. To me, that has always been the key to Dylan's art. To state things plainly is the function of journalism; but Dylan sings a more fugitive song: allusive, symbolic, full of imagery and ellipses, and by leaving things out, he allows us the grand privilege of creating along with him. His song becomes our song because we live in those spaces . . . we fill up the mystery, we expand and inhabit the work of art."
—Pete Hamill

Liner Notes for *Blood on the Tracks* (1974)

DAVID GAHR

STUART BRATESMAN

The tour is also a tremendous success. In Chicago, Hollywood, Memphis, New York City, Denver, Oakland, Los Angeles, and elsewhere — Dylan and The Band work magic on spellbound audiences, many of whom appear to be having something akin to a religious experience. Fans of his own generation — now in their thirties — relive the sixties and take stock of their own lives *vis-a-vis* Dylan's maturing point of view; new fans are dazzled by his intensity and the power of his musical performance.

JOSEPH SIA

"Tough Mama" is a hard-rock boogie with a terrific beat, greatly enhanced by the solid presence of The Band on back-up. Dylan has written songs to Mama before, sometimes confusing the mother with her daughter so there's a clear sexual link among the three—or maybe two of them are only one, as in this case: this Mama is also referred to and adored as the Dark Beauty, the Sweet Goddess, and a Silver Angel. Jesus, what a woman this must be to provoke such homage. Dylan here expresses his great respect for the lady, his love and appreciation, plus some awe and even a little fear. This woman is impressive, and she's been around:

Sweet Goddess
Born of a blinding light and a
changing wind
Now, don't be modest
You know who you are and where
you've been.

This woman is so strong, so powerful, she clearly has the balance of power, leaving a begrudging, plaintive Dylan down on his knees, "grateful" if she'd take his ring. Yes, there are some strange glimmerings of a complex relationship here; this is no simple romantic ballad. There also appears to be some reference to other men in the lady's past:

Jack, the Cowboy, went up north
He's buried in your past
The Lone Wolf went out drinking
That was over pretty fast.

Moreover the singer pulls rank when he says

It's my duty
To bring you down to the field where
the flowers bloom . . . .

. . . as if he could exert the prerogatives of a proud possessor or a lord or a

FRED W. McDARRAH

husband. There's a struggle of some kind going on here, a variation on the infinite, never-ending battle of the sexes. Dylan has expressed his bitterness, anger, and desire for revenge before, but never so subtly, never with such resolution to win this hard skirmish and ride off in final union:

I'm crestfallen
The world of illusion is at my door. . . .
I ain't a-haulin'
Any of my lambs to the market place
anymore
The prison walls are crumblin'
There is no end in sight
I've gained some recognition
But I lost my appetite
Dark Beauty
Meet me at the border late tonight.

The words here are mightily aided and abetted by the tight punchy rhythm and nervous beat. What a complex song for a man to sing to a woman! How *many* feelings are snapped around here like a rubber band on his lover's flesh: admiration, jealousy, bitterness, love, determination to hold on. . . .

"Hazel" breaks the intensity. Dylan gives us a breather, pacing the songs so we don't fall out with psychic exhaustion, providing something sweet and simple, almost like a children's song, before plunging ahead again with "Something There Is About You." This solemn hymn is yet a more avid tribute to his lover, yet a more straightforward and sincere expression of his profound debt to this person. And what a lover this is, what a mysterious, powerful creature:

Something there is about you
That strikes a match in me. . . .
Or is it because you remind me
Of somethin' that used to be
Something that's crossed over
From another country.

This person, he says, has been responsible for his survival and for the meaning and purpose of his life. But then there's that ambivalence creeping in, that strange sense of paradox we first encountered in "Tough Mama." He sings:

I could say that I'd be faithful
I could say it in one sweet, easy breath.
But to you that would be cruelty
And to me it surely would be death.

> "His whole concept of making an album seemed to be go ahead and play it and whichever way it comes out well that's the way it is. It's what happens at the moment. He didn't want to do a lot of takes and I don't blame him 'cause some of the songs are so long. We'd just watch his hands and pray we had the right changes."
> —Charlie Brown

Electric Guitarist for Deliverance on recording *Blood on the Tracks,* in *Rolling Stone*

DAVID GAHR

Sounds like star-crossed lovers, in the tragic tradition of Romeo and Juliet. On the one hand he adores this person but he also seems to be spacing himself away (cf. "Going Going Gone"), giving himself some distance as if to protect himself from what might become fatal.

Side One of *Planet Waves* now ends with one of the cast-iron works promised above: an anthem and a prayer and an exhortation to the divine entitled "Forever Young." Garth Hudson's organ helps this sound like a hymn, like "Father of Night." This hymn is a blessing from a father to his own children, in the patriarchal biblical tradition:

May your hands always be busy
May your feet always be swift
May you have a strong foundation
When the winds of changes shift
May your heart always be joyful
May your song always be sung
May you stay forever young.

Sing that out loud around the dinner table next Thanksgiving, or at a Seder, if you have one. What a fine catalog of blessings Father Dylan here intones. Singing this across the country during that tour in 1974, how Dylan moved his audience, many of whom were either parents themselves by now or younger than Dylan, a new generation of fans and disciples come to sit at the feet of a teacher.

Side two opens with a completely different version of the same song, "Forever Young." Whereas the first take was slow and serious, this second rendition is a hillbilly, red-neck version sung in a completely different, highly accented, nasal twanging voice. Faster, lighter, and less ponderous, there's a startling difference in this hokey-hoedown version, which nicely balances the previous version. But you could perform this song a dozen different ways, and it would still work, it would still be an inspiration and a blessing to receive.

"Dirge" continues the biblical tone of this album. True to its title, the music is funereal, with a sad Latin guitar accompanied by an ominous progression of minor chords on the piano. Very bleak. Very mournful, a song of misspent passion, bad love, about guilt and playing foolish games:

I hate myself for lovin' you
And the weakness that it showed
You were just a painted face
On a trip down Suicide Road. . . .

It's like a flipside of "Like a Rolling

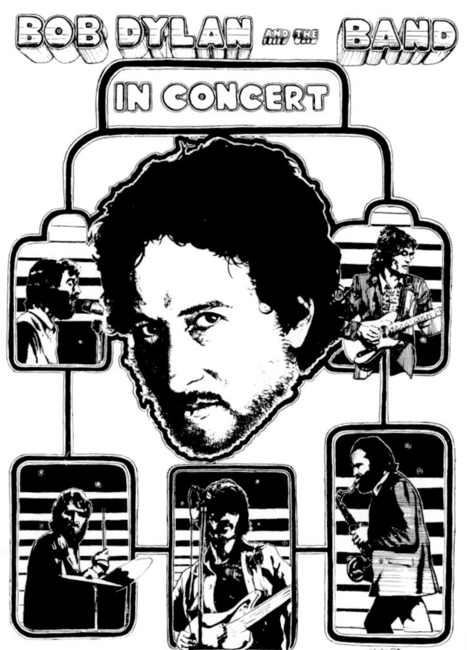

Asylum releases a double-record set of live performances made during the tour, specifically on January 30 (at Madison Square Garden) and on February 13 and February 14 (at The Forum in Los Angeles).

Summer 1974. **Having fulfilled his two-record obligation to Elektra/Asylum with *Planet Waves* and *Before the Flood,* Dylan does not renew this contract but rather signs again with his old company, Columbia. Terms of his renegotiated agreement are rumored to include a retroactive raise in royalties for all of his albums, as well as the reversion of ownership of his master tapes to Dylan after a period of five years—both exceptional concessions.**

CHUCK PULIN

Stone," but whereas in that missive he berates his former lover and antagonist, in "Dirge" he's flagellating himself for being such a fool—for having such weakness and wasting himself so. Both songs are bitter and vindictive, but this time out, years later, Dylan saves his greatest venom for himself, and it's truly savage:

I hate that foolish game we played
And the need that was expressed. . . .
I hate myself for lovin' you
But I should get over that.

Dylan's experience and understanding of love has grown in complexity. It

This valedictory "Wedding Song" is the most confessional and explicit of them all, exposing most profoundly the singer's hunger, his continuing yearning *and* his anxiety.

I love you more than ever
More than time and more than love . . .
Love you more than madness . . .
Love you more than life itself . . .

Dylan delivers this entreaty like a cantor praying to God in the synagogue, twisting and turning around the notes and phrases, precisely and deliberately, in his Middle Eastern, wailing style:

> "I want to lay down a whole bunch of tracks. I don't want to overdub. I want it easy and natural."
> —Bob Dylan
>
> To John Hammond before recording *Blood on the Tracks*

now ranges from hot and horny to bitter and self-loathing.

"You Angel You" is another adulatory love song, less convincing than some of the other "torches" on this record, a bit lighter and delivered in a flatter vocal style. The lover and subject of the song is depicted as a "heavenly child," and the singer can't sleep, walks the floor, wants more and more. This love sounds like a terrible *pain,* a theme reiterated in the next song "Never Say Goodbye" (not to be confused with the Isaac Hayes-Jackson Five number "Never Can Say Goodbye"). This is a far more interesting song musically, with Rick Danko's bass holding it all together, sweet and stirring. Again, it has a strident, almost desperate clinging quality. It's an overstated anthem, frought with intense pressure, hunger, and pleading.

You're beautiful beyond words
You're beautiful to me
You can make me cry
Never say goodbye . . . .

He can't live without her, she's saved him and sacrificed herself. He's weak, vulnerable, needy, waiting for her to come grab hold of his hand. What a woman! And she's changed her last name, too.

"Wedding Song" is an appropriately chosen finale for the record and also a fitting conclusion to one of the album's major themes. Nine out of ten songs on *Planet Waves* are love songs, and a great deal of what they convey is gratitude coupled with desperation.

When I was deep in poverty
You taught me how to give. . . .

Dylan wants to say how grateful he is:

You gave me babies, one, two, three
What is more, you saved my life. . . .

But there's a primitive, primordial side to this passion which is frightening:

Eye for eye and tooth for tooth
Your love cuts like a knife . . .

JOSEPH SIA

What's lost is lost, we can't regain
What went down in the flood
But happiness to me is you
And I love you more than blood.

These two have been through pain together, disruption, separation—the wounds they've given each other still smart, and it's scary how Dylan pleads to hang on:

Oh, can't you see that you were born
To stand by my side.

The way he sings, "Oh, *can't* you see" the demand, the old possessiveness ("to *stand by my side"*). We've all felt this. Our salvation, too, has depended on the love of another. Dylan's music, his words, his intense, dramatic, punching, biting, whining, enunciating, cajoling singing—they express our need, too. But it's alarming to recognize yourself in a song that says:

Cause I love you more than ever
Now that the past is gone.

That line about the past sounds like whistling in the dark. We believe his passion and his need; we worry about the future. These sentiments express a turning point, a desire for reaffirmation and renewal. Perhaps that's why he's asking for a new commitment, a second WEDDING. In any case, he's laid out the hardships of a long-term, painfully sustained loving relationship.

Dylan has come a long way from the confidence and serenity of *Nashville Skyline* and *New Morning.* Those rosy-colored love songs were much simpler and happier. There's been a change now, four years later: malaise, hunger, jealousy, and sadness burn throughout these torch ballads.

Planet Waves was recorded in three days. Only three songs—"Going Going Gone," "On a Night like This," and "Never Say Goodbye"—required overdubbing. In an age when months of studio work and electronic wizardry are the norm, Dylan's quickness and economy are remarkable. Dylan eschews gimmickry and overelaborate production methods. In this case, especially, he knew what he wanted to say, and he *said it.* After a relatively long silence, he's given us a progress report, a state of the artist, a consolidated self-portrait of his mind and feelings and his intentions—his ambitions to renew, to continue his quest, to reiterate his moral and spiritual positions even more adamantly. Sober, determined, still hopeful in loving, he rides out again to do battle in his own life and to share, teach, exhort, and inspire us to do the same.

Before the Flood

Asylum Records AB-201. Recording Engineers: Phil Ramone/Rob Fraboni. Released July 1974. Most Likely You Go Your Way (and I'll Go Mine), Lay Lady Lay, Rainy Day Women #12 & 35, Knockin' on Heaven's Door, It Ain't Me, Babe, Ballad of a Thin Man (*All written by B. Dylan*); Up on Cripple Creek (*Robertson*), I Shall Be Released (*Dylan*), Endless Highway (*Robertson*), The Night They Drove Old Dixie Down (*Robertson*), Stage Fright (*Robertson*); Don't Think Twice, It's All Right (*Dylan*), Just Like a Woman (*Dylan*), It's Alright, Ma (I'm Only Bleeding) (*Dylan*), The Shape I'm In (*Robertson*), When You Awake (*Robertson and Manuel*), The Weight (*Robertson*); All Along the Watchtower, Highway 61 Revisited, Like a Rolling Stone, Blowin' in the Wind. (*B. Dylan*).

As if to celebrate this return to the fold, Dylan goes straight into Columbia's New York studios with a bunch of new songs he's been writing. He's prepared himself carefully, on his own. Now, at the last minute, a group of great musicians is gathered together on the spur of the moment for a spontaneous session. Professionals like Buddy Cage, Eric Weissberg, Charlie Brown, and Deliverance — who had a hit with "Dueling Banjos" — are slick enough to follow his lead and fill in the musical spaces wherever he leads them. In a remarkably short time, the new album — ominously titled *Blood on the Tracks* — is recorded and released by Columbia.

With Dennis Hopper, Arlo Guthrie, Melvin Van Peebles (partially obscured), Melanie and Dave Von Ronk at the Chile Benefit in Madison Square Garden

WIDE WORLD PHOTOS

LETHAL DOSE OF LOVE

BOB
DYLAN
BLOOD
ON
THE
TRACKS

Blood on the Tracks

Columbia PC 33235. Engineered by Phil Ramone. Released 1974. Tangled Up in Blue, Simple Twist of Fate, You're a Big Girl Now, Idiot Wind, You're Gonna Make Me Lonesome When You Go; Meet Me in the Morning, Lily, Rosemary and the Jack of Hearts, If You See Her, Say Hello, Shelter from the Storm, Buckets of Rain (*All by Bob Dylan*).

CHUCK PULIN

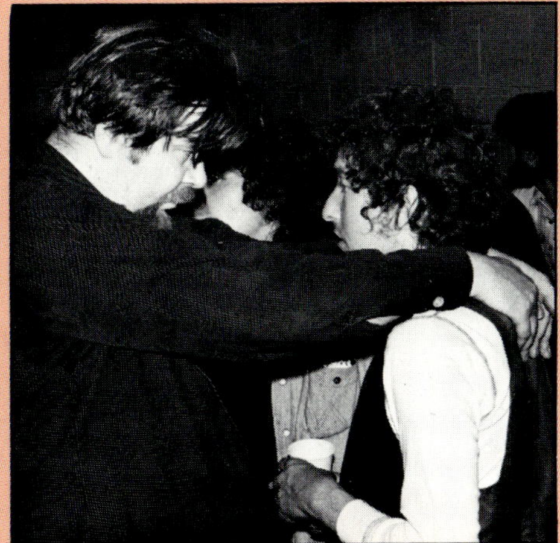

CHUCK PULIN

If ever an album was appropriately titled, it's *Blood on the Tracks.* There's blood all over the album. Blood bannered down the left-hand side of the front-cover art flat up against an abstract, almost pointillistic photograph of Dylan. The specter of blood splattered all over his face, through his hair, at the back of his head. Blood red bleeding behind the credits and the excellent liner notes by Pete Hamill on the back of the album. And lots of blood, Dylan's blood flowing over and through every track, every song sung on this record.

It's ironic. Dylan has always tried to hide himself. He doesn't go on talk shows or give very many interviews. He's a very, very private person who's guarded his personal life and his family from the public eye with a determination bordering on fanaticism. And yet he reveals himself enormously in his music, he takes off his psychic clothing before our very eyes and ears, peeling away the masks and defenses and—especially in this album—exposing the raw feelings, the nerves and sinews.

Blood on the Tracks could have been subtitled *Love's Labor Lost.* For whereas *Planet Waves,* released earlier the same year, was about hanging on to love, *Blood on the Tracks* takes place after the fall. The overwhelming theme of nearly every song on the record is lost love, breaking up, the dissolution of a very important relationship. What distinguishes this album from both other work on the same subject and from Dylan's previous love songs is that this group of ballads all approach the same subject from a variety of disparate angles. Dylan reacts to a cataclysmic event with all the complexity it deserves: he's mad, he's resigned, he's vindictive, he's forgiving, he's hurt and bitter, he's playful and ironic, he's understanding—he doesn't understand, he's filled with rage and frustration, he's philosophical, he's content, he's discontent. This album is a *tour de force* on the subject of breaking up

CHUCK PULIN

with someone, someone with whom you've shared a whole lot of your life, someone who's always going to be very important, forever in your consciousness.

"Tangled up in Blue" opens the album with a survey of the relationship, an overview, a history of how it started, the early years and good stuff, the changes and hardships and disillusion, the falling apart. It's complicated and it's sad, it's *blue*. There's a powerful feeling of loss, of feeling and events getting out of control:

And when finally the bottom fell out
I became withdrawn
The only thing I knew how to do
Was to keep on keepin' on . . . .

Things don't work out but on the last verse, he's still hopeful:

So now I'm goin' back again
I got to get to her somehow . . . .

The song ends with him "still on the road, heading for another joint." Will he find her? Can they ever get back to where they were?

"Simple Twist of Fate" tells another sad tale of loss and regret. A slight reverberating echo on the vocal, combined with a haunting F#m chord after the first line of every verse, helps to give this song a melancholy aspect. As in "Tangled up in Blue," this affair heated up to a glow but then inexplicably died:

They sat together in the park
As the evening sky grew dark
She looked at him and he felt a spark
Tingle to his bone
'Twas then he felt alone
And wished that he'd gone straight
And watched out for a simple twist of fate.

What did he do wrong? Why at the very moment of contact between them, does he feel alone? Do we really expect a simple answer? Haven't we also experienced that separation when it's what we've wanted least? Again, Dylan asks the right questions. As in so many of his songs since "Blowin' in the Wind," he anatomizes our universal dilemma, presenting us with the paradoxes and contradictions and accidents of life—of fate. This man had a great chance, held it briefly, and lost it. Why didn't it work out? Who knows? Twists and tangles and terrible caprice! In any case, he's not saying. But, he hopes for her still, for her return and their reunion . . .

Maybe she'll pick him out again
How long must he wait
Once more for a simple twist of fate . . . .

Other artists have recorded this song, finding in it a vehicle for saying so much about love: the vivid portrait of doomed romance, the awful feeling of helplessness and sorrow.

"You're a Big Girl Now" goes beyond separation and hope for reunion to some real remorse, complete with a recurring wail, a mournful cry that's repeated emphatically in the middle of each verse. "Oh-oh," he cries, "Oooooh-ooooooh!" BANG, the song begins with this conversation, "short and sweet," sounds like so-long, "it nearly swept me off-a my feet." This lover has put him out "back in the rain," she has the upper hand here as the plaintive singer bemoans the split:

Oh, but what a shame
If all we've shared can't last
I can change, I swear
Oh-oh . . .

He'll reform. He'll even overcome his jealousy:

Oh, I know where I can find you
Oh-oh
In somebody's room
It's a price I have to pay
You're a big girl all the way.

All this is delivered quite sincerely, slowly, deliberately. It's an amazing piece of self-exposure. "I can change, *I swear*" he sings against those two guitars and the piano chording and the tense rat-tatting of the drumsticks on the edge of the snare. How can you get a line like that out of your head? How many times have we thought that or said it to someone we've loved? And the final plea is

But what's the sense of changing
Horses in midstream

CHUCK PULIN

I'm going out of my mind
Oh-oh . . .

"Idiot Wind" presents a different side of the same story. There's no instrumental introduction, nossir, it starts right in with a savage burst of energy: "Someone's got it in for me . . . ." Is that clear? Can you get the message: they're telling lies and even his "sweet lady" had "to ask me where it was at, I couldn't believe after all these years, You didn't know me any better than that." Dylan's mad in this faster, more violent diatribe against IDIOTS who spread rumors about him. And who's he yelling at? Someone in the media who's been spreading lies about him; a personal friend who's betrayed him with fallacious gossip; a lover who's turned on him with a vengeance? Whoever it was, they were close once and now they're miles apart. Something just awful has happened between them and he's mad as hell, vindictive, nasty:

Idiot wind
Blowing every time ya move your teeth
You're an idiot, babe
It's a wonder that you still know how to breathe.

The answer sure isn't blowin' in this particular wind. On the contrary, Dylan feels betrayed, double-crossed, and misled by misspent passion and devotion. In stark contrast to the regret of the previous songs and the desire for reunion, he now curses the day he ever trusted or loved this person:

You tamed the lion in my cage
But it just wasn't enough to change my heart. . . .

BUT . . . but in verse number four, the last verse of the song, he shows us even more of his vulnerability; he goes beyond just anger and hurting to show us how he blames himself, too, because what's true against her can be true against him, too:

You'll never know the hurt I suffered
Nor the pain I rise above
And I'll never know the same about you
Your holiness or your kind of love
An' it makes me feel
So sorry.

So that at the conclusion he's calling himself an idiot, too. He confesses in blunt, hard-chosen words that he has to blame them both:

Idiot wind
Blowing through the buttons of our coats
Blowing through the letters that we wrote . . .
We're idiots, babe
It's a wonder we can even feed ourselves.

"*Our* coats . . . *we* wrote . . . *our*selves . . ." And what a feeling of revulsion to provoke this inversion of the very words he used in his earliest masterpiece.

The first side of the album concludes with "You're Gonna Make Me Lonesome When You Go," a quick and almost jolly number that Dylan sings in his sly, folksy, gremlin sort of voice, touching on these grave matters very lightly this time around, saying all these terrible things in the gentlest, aw-shucks, and gee-whillikers sort of manner. The situation is actually the same: things ain't what they should be, "When somethin's not right, it's wrong," he sings, confessing that this has been the most important relationship in his life so far, that nothing he's experienced can equal this love. But he says all this whimsically, humorously, in a self-deprecating tone:

Situations have ended sad
Relationships have all been bad
Mine've been like Verlaine's and Rimbaud

_1975._ For years bootleg recordings and tapes of unreleased Dylan material have surfaced in great quantities throughout the world. The most widespread and respected of these unauthorized albums is _The Basement Tapes,_ a bootleg release of several home recordings which Dylan made with The Band from June to October in 1967, a short time before _John Wesley Harding._ Originally taped with a small machine and only three mikes in the basement of the house called The Big Pink, these recordings feature Dylan making high-spirited, fraternal music with Robbie Robertson, Richard Manuel, Rick Danko, Garth Hudson, and Levon Helm. The songs are so good, the bootleg so popular —Columbia finally remasters these home recordings with Dylan's consent and cooperation and releases the legendary _Basement Tapes_ as an official two-disk album.

THE
BASEMENT
TAPES

But there's no way I can compare
All those scenes to this affair
Yer gonna make me lonesome when
you go.

A charming song. A jolly performance. But the irony gap is horrendous. The stark, even tragic content grapples with the cunning, stiff-upper-lip style—and this tension touches our hearts.

"Meet Me in the Morning" opens the second side with a solid, good beat delivered in a high Dylan black voice. It's a blues number, again about lost love. Dylan's been done in, hurt and left behind once more. This time he and he keeps on getting better.

The three concluding songs on the album return to its original theme of separation and lost love. "If You See Her, Say Hello" is a paragon of respect and understanding for a lover who's left him:

I always have respected her
For busting out and gettin' free
Oh whatever makes her happy
I won't stand in the way. . . .

How's that for wisdom and restraint? Here, at least for the moment, he's able to honor his former love and to distance himself from the pain he's felt:

> Neither *John Wesley Harding*, made later that year, nor *Music from Big Pink* (for which all of The Band's numbers here were at one time intended), sound much like *The Basement Tapes*, but there are two elements the three sessions do share: a feeling of age, a kind of classicism; and an absolute commitment by the singers and musicians to their material. Beneath the easy rolling surface of *The Basement Tapes* there is some serious business going on. What was taking shape, as Dylan and The Band fiddled with the tunes, was less a style than a spirit—a spirit that had to do with a delight in friendship and invention.
> —Greil Marcus

On the liner notes to *The Basement Tapes* © 1975 by CBS Inc.

feels "so exposed" and abandoned and wretched, struggling through "barbed wire," outrunning hound dogs to be with a woman who nonetheless turns him down. This downtrodden dirge is followed by the epic ballad "Lily, Rosemary and the Jack of Hearts"—a very long (eight minutes and fifty seconds) narrative tale which employs only three simple major chords and about sixteen verses to tell a richly complex story, which could be a scenario for a novel or a film. It's a western, a classic tale of the mysterious stranger, the Jack of Hearts, who comes to town and robs the bank. Two women love this outlaw. One kills for him and is hanged as the Jack of Hearts rides off with "quite a haul." The surprise twists in the plot, the language, the sexual tension, the enigmatic, charismatic hero—all sustain a wonderful dramatic tension in this ballad, which makes it as much fun to experience as *High Noon* or *The Threepenny Opera*. Dylan's becoming a master at this sort of narrative song,

And I've never gotten used to it
I've just learned to turn it off
Either I'm too sensitive
Or else I'm gettin' soft.

Dylan's putting bandages on his wounds here, but the blood still shows through. This is all very mature and controlled, but there's some terrible remorse breaking through and some glimmers of ever-so-faint lingering hope:

I replay the past
I know every scene by heart. . . .
If she's passin' back this way
I'm not that hard to find
Tell her she can look me up
If she's got the time.

"Shelter from the Storm" returns to a description of love's beginnings. More overt, less symbolic than "Tangled up in Blue," Dylan sings here of man saved by woman, of salvation through love:

I came in from the wilderness
A creature void of form. . . .
She walked up to me so gracefully
And took my crown of thorns. . . .
"Come in," she said, "I'll give you
Shelter from the storm."

Dylan has gone over this a million times in his head, trying to figure what went wrong:

Now there's a wall between us
Something there's been lost
I took too much for granted
Got my signals crossed. . . .

If only he could turn back the clock, if only he could recapture the first flush, the original flash, that magic.

"Buckets of Rain" is one of Dylan's best valedictory songs, carefully chosen to bring down the curtain on this album. It's a warm, gentle, loving, tender song, tempered by the continuing strong sense of loss and melancholy. Dylan still has a lot of love in him, and he's ready to spend it. He's suffered, he's been burned, he's got emotional baggage: buckets of tears and buckets of blood, too. But he's willing to take another chance.

I been meek and hard like an oak
I seen pretty people disappear like
smoke
Friends will arrive
Friends will disappear
If you want me
Honey baby, I'll be here.

So after ten songs and nearly fifty minutes of sustained exposition on the subject of broken hearts, Dylan leaves us finally with a song of hope. Faint hope, perhaps, but hope nonetheless. It may work out, it may not, but it's worth a crack. Hell, it's all there is. . . .

Life is sad, life is a bust
All you can do is do what you must
You do what you must do
And ya do it well
I'll do it for you
Honey baby, can't you tell.

"Buckets of Rain" is a short song, neat and concise, with an excellent, plain guitar accompaniment. It concludes our lesson for today with cautious optimism, resignation, acceptance, and still—overall—belief in the saving power of love.

Ultimately, then, this is an inspirational album. The message is survival, is loving in the teeth of hurt, is sadder but wiser tenderness and renewed devotion. It's a fine message to carry with you. "Justice so moves that those only learn who suffer." Aeschylus said that. "I bargained for salvation, An' they gave me a lethal dose." Dylan said that. And who said, "Only women bleed"?

The Basement Tapes

Columbia C2 33682. Compiled by Robbie Robertson. Produced by Bob Dylan and The Band. Recorded in the basement of Big Pink, West Saugerties, N.Y., 1967. Released 1975. Odds and Ends (*B. Dylan*), Orange Juice Blues (Blues for Breakfast) (*R. Manuel*), Million Dollar Bash (*B. Dylan*), Yazoo Street Scandal (*J. R. Robertson*), Going to Acapulco (*B. Dylan*), Katie's Been Gone (*J. R. Robertson, R. Manuel*); Lo and Behold (*B. Dylan*), Bessie Smith (*R. Danko, J. R. Robertson*), Clothes Line Saga (*B. Dylan*), Apple Suckling Tree (*B. Dylan*), Please, Mrs. Henry (*B. Dylan*), Tears of Rage (*B. Dylan, R. Manuel*); Too Much of Nothing (*B. Dylan*), Yea! Heavy and a Bottle of Bread (*B. Dylan*), Ain't No More Cane (*Traditional, Arranged by The Band*), Crash on the Levee (Down in the Flood) (*B. Dylan*), Ruben Remus (*J. R. Robertson, R. Manuel*), Tiny Montgomery (*B. Dylan*); You Ain't Goin' Nowhere (*B. Dylan*), Don't Ya Tell Henry (*B. Dylan*), Nothing Was Delivered (*B. Dylan*), Open the Door, Homer (*B. Dylan*), Long Distance Operator (*B. Dylan*), This Wheel's on Fire (*B. Dylan, R. Danko*).

***1975* (continued). Dylan undertakes to champion the cause of Rubin "Hurricane" Carter, a former number-one contender for the middleweight boxing crown, who has been incarcerated for nine years in the New Jersey state penitentiary for a triple murder he says he didn't commit. Carter's conviction had been based on the accusations of two police informers who have since recanted their testimony. Consequently Dylan and others launch a National Defense Fund to release the ex-fighter on bail and get him a new trial. As part of this effort, Dylan records a hit single called "Hurricane," which also leads off another major new album of political and personal songs entitled *Desire*.**

LYNN GOLDSMITH

REDEMPTION

PC 33893
Columbia
BOB DYLAN
DESIRE

Desire

Columbia PC 33893. "This record could have been produced by Don DeVito." Released 1975. Hurricane (*B. Dylan, J. Levy*), Isis (*B. Dylan, J. Levy*), Mozambique (*B. Dylan, J. Levy*), One More Cup of Coffee (*B. Dylan*), Oh, Sister (*B. Dylan, J. Levy*); Joey (*B. Dylan, J. Levy*), Romance in Durango (*B. Dylan, J. Levy*), Black Diamond Bay (*B. Dylan, J. Levy*), Sara (*B. Dylan*).

LYNN GOLDSMITH

This is my favorite album. Many prefer Dylan's earliest recordings: *The Freewheelin' Bob Dylan, Bringing It All Back Home,* and the rocker *Blonde on Blonde*. Others like Dylan's middle period of piety and conjugal bliss and, yes, *John Wesley Harding, Nashville Skyline,* and *New Morning* are wonderful to hear, so sure and warm and happy, like fond old friends from our salad years. But let's not get stuck back there in the good old days when we were young, and everything was new. Let's keep up with Dylan's third phase, which begins with *Planet Waves,* through *Blood on the Tracks* and now, on to *Desire.* Because these records represent the most fully realized expressions of a great artist in his maturity. Because *Desire,* more than anything that has come before, explodes with Dylan's openhearted power in a rich variety of virtuoso styles over a broad spectrum of deeply felt emotions, flights of illumination, universal fantasy, and personal, gut-issue messages—from his heart to ours.

Dylan's greatness has always been his ability to express what we are experiencing; adolescent rebellion, sociopolitical apocalypticism and rampant naivetē, hot fucks, perhaps children, love paranoia, crazy speed, consciousness catapulting, hurt, rejection, the breakup of an important relationship or two, death nearby and coming closer, self-realization leading to doubt, ambivalence, vulnerability, compassion, empathy, diversity, flexibility, alternatives. *Desire* expresses all this; the album, the songs, the metaphor—the great East Indian holy men say we are all living now in the Desire World, that everything we do and feel is motivated by DESIRE.

***March 23, 1975.* Dylan appears at Bill Graham's S.N.A.C.K. Benefit concert for athletics, culture and kicks for San Francisco students.**

LYNN GOLDSMITH

Above: With Bette Midler

MICHAEL ZAGARIS

Freud said something like that, too, and certainly all the passions and issues on this album come from desire: for freedom and justice, for love, salvation, and fulfillment. But there's a subtitle to this album: *Songs of Redemption.* An interesting choice of words for a man who chooses his words very carefully. Redemption means to buy back, to liberate by payment, or on a more spiritual level, to free from the bondage of sin, to change for the better or REFORM; or, heavier yet, to atone for or expiate. Once again, as in "My Back Pages" and "I Am a Lonesome Hobo," Dylan seems to be in a mood for self-criticism, for paying some dues, for reevaluating his prior positions, and exposing his own process of change.

The musical arrangements on this album are wonderful, particularly the use of the violin, played in a haunting gypsy style by a young woman named Scarlet Rivera, whom Dylan is rumored to have met on the street in Greenwich Village. Ronee Blakeley and EmmyLou Harris—both star vocalists on their own—are outstanding on background vocals, and there's also effective, original, unusual use of the accordion by Dom Cortese and the Bellzouki by Vincent Bell. In each instance, with each song, Dylan also sets the piece in a kind of theatrical style. His performance throughout this album is like a series of numbers from a cabaret or a Kurt Weill/Bertolt Brecht piece of musical theater. Many of the songs were co-written with Jacques Levy, a writer-director-actor with a strong theatrical background, and Dylan's own enunciation, his different voices and disguises and disparate persona on this record represent some of his best acting ever.

The album opens with a bang: *"Pistol shots ring out in the barroom night. . . ."* It's "Hurricane," Dylan's one-man successful effort to get a retrial for Hurricane Carter, a former contender for the middleweight boxing crown, who appeared to have

ALVAN MEYEROWITZ

> **"I'm a firm believer in the longer you live, the better you get.—Bob Dylan"**

From *Conversations with Bob Dylan* by John Cohen and Happy Traum, *Sing Out!* 1968

CHUCK KRALL

been framed for murder. It's an eleven-verse ballad, a tight little mini-drama you can't stop listening to. The music is driving, compelling. Dylan's performance is like a jackhammer, snapping and biting out the words with passion and vicious irony. It's more powerful than "Hollis Brown." And it's wonderful to see Dylan return to a form that his critics had bemoaned as obsolete ("What? A *protest* song?") and produce something even better than before:

Not all the criminals in their coats and their ties
Are free to drink martinis and watch the sun rise
While Rubin sits like Buddha in a ten-foot cell
An innocent man in a living hell.

And it worked. The song made it a good way up the AM charts as a single, Carter did get a retrial and, ironically, was found guilty again and returned to his cell.

"Isis" is a humorous novella, cowritten with Jacques Levy, set in a leisurely, romantic, three-quarter tempo. It's a funny but sad tale of fatal attraction for a mysterious woman, a goddess the narrator marries but cannot hold or live with. Like many a poor lover before him, he goes off on a quest for some kind of Holy Grail on her behalf:

I was think' about turquoise, I was think' about gold,
I was think' about diamonds and the world's biggest necklace.

After many hardships and the death of his partner, he returns "just to tell her I love her," only to find her cool, indifferent, he's not even sure she wants him around anymore:

Isis, oh, Isis, you mystical child.
What drives me to you is what drives me insane.

> "Later on the songs got more defined, but it didn't necessarily bring more power to them. The sound was whatever happened to be available at the time. . . . I just haven't paid as much attention to it as I should have. I haven't felt comfortable in a studio since I worked with Tom Wilson . . . my recording sessions have tended to be last-minute affairs. I don't really use all the technical studio stuff. My songs are done live in the studio; they always have been and they always will be done that way. That's why they're alive. No matter what else you say about them, they are alive. —Bob Dylan"
>
> To Ron Rosenbaum, © 1978 by *Playboy*

RICHARD McCAFFREE

Ah, women! Will he ever figure them out? Will men and women ever get together? Will men ever please women? Will women ever need men as much as men need women? Or will men like Bob Dylan ever want the kind of woman who needs him as much as he needs her?

"Mozambique" lives up to the exotic flavor of its name. This song has a kind of Hollywood mombo-bombo beat with congas and EmmyLou Harris in a high, high harmony. Very romantic, very sensual, a hot little story of quick passion in tropical languor:

MICHAEL ZAGARIS

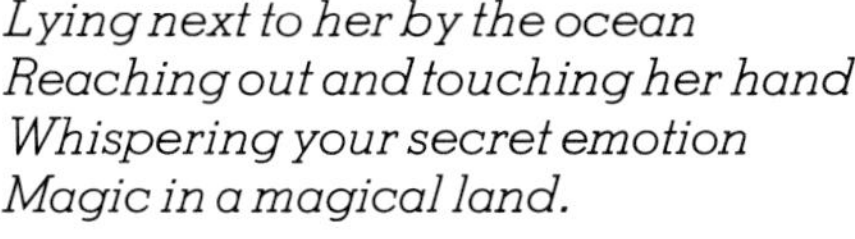

Lying next to her by the ocean
Reaching out and touching her hand
Whispering your secret emotion
Magic in a magical land.

It's so sexy, you want to take the next plane and fly off straightway down there with the honey of your choice. It's the opposite side of the coin from "Isis," which in its allegorical way describes the frustrating reality of relationships between men and women. No, "Mozambique" falls over us like manna from heaven, the way it can be very rarely but should be all the time: utter romance and total contact—all set in tropical paradise. Nice work if you can get it.

"One More Cup of Coffee (Valley Below)" was written by Dylan alone. It sounds like a cross between a cantor singing Kol Nidre and a gypsy singing to his horse high in the mountains. A violin, as played by Scarlet Rivera, provides prominent counterpoint, which gives the whole piece a haunting, melancholy power, evoking all

KRISTIN SUNBOM

Photos from SNACK benefit in San Francisco. Below: Sara Dylan

MICHAEL ZAGARIS

the pain and frustration and sorrow of this sad relationship between a man and a woman:

. . . I don't sense affection
No gratitude or love
Your loyalty is not to me
But to the stars above.

Again, the woman has power over him. Again, she's aloof and indifferent to his love. He's tried everything, and it hasn't worked. It just ain't him that can give her everything that she wants: he's *not* the most important thing to her. . . . But how he loves her still:

Your voice is like a meadow lark
But your heart is like an ocean
Mysterious and dark. . . .

So he's having one more cup for the road. Then: he's leaving. What can a man do?

This album can be taken as a reply to Carol King's *Tapestry.* That best-selling album, and particularly the song "It's Too Late Baby," was a revolutionary, liberating anthem for many women in the early 1970's. *Desire*—particularly the songs "One More Cup of Coffee" and the next cut "Oh, Sister"—express a man's reaction to women's anger, hurt, breaking out, putting down, and getting free of men. In "Oh, Sister" Dylan says it's too damn bad we can't get along better because we're meant for each other, we're related, God wanted it this way and dammit, we should *not* be strangers or enemies. And as if to prove such harmony is possible, Dylan again (as in "One More Cup of Coffee") has EmmyLou Harris singing right along with him in perfect thirds, perfect fifths, perfect sympathy, sweet and complementary all the way.

"Oh, Sister" is a jewel of precision and comprehension. Within three short verses and a brief refrain, Dylan conveys the real reason for "desire": it's God's will. We were made for each other. Naturally. We mustn't go against this, for only madness and danger can follow such disruption:

Oh, sister when I come to lie in your
arms,
You should not treat me like a stranger
Our Father would not like the way that
you act,
And you must realize The danger.

This is a plea for reunion, for an end to the battle of the sexes. **Enough!** Dylan cries. **Stop!** We are brothers and sisters. Blood relations. We've got to **get back together.** The music is slow and steady, four-four time, dirgelike and plaintive, didactic, preachy, dead serious, and deeply moving.

110

1975 (*continued*). Dylan goes back on the road with a completely different kind of tour, which he calls the Rolling Thunder Revue. Rather than play formal concerts at large halls and coliseums, he assembles a loosely knit merry group of old friends to make an informal, low-keyed, unpublicized tour of the Northeast. For several months, Joan Baez, Jack Elliot, Phil Ochs, Bobby Neuwirth, Sam Shepard, Roger McGuinn, Arlo Guthrie, Allen Ginsberg, Joni Mitchell, Ronee Blakeley, and others join Dylan's band (T-Bone Burnett, Howie Wyeth, Rob Stoner, Luther Rix, Steve Soles, and Scarlet Rivera) in a series of thirty impromptu performances in twenty-two towns and small cities.

The notion is to have some fun and make some music in an unstructured free-floating environment. Dylan also engages a film crew to record everything that's happening both on and off the stage throughout the tour.

CHUCK PULIN

Photo: With Patti Smith in the Village.

"In the early period, I was writing more about objection, obsession or rejection. Superimposing my own reality on that which seemed to have no reality of its own. . . . The goddess isn't real. A pretty woman as a goddess is just up there on a pedestal. The flower is what we are really concerned about here. The opening and the closing, the growth, the bafflement. You don't lust after flowers. . . . I don't single out women as anything to get hung up about. . . . The real magic of women is that throughout the ages, they've had to do all the work and yet they can have a sense of humor. —Bob Dylan"

To Ron Rosenbaum, © 1978 by *Playboy*

JOSEPH SIA

December 9, 1975. Dylan and his Rolling Thunder Revue sell out Madison Square Garden for their final performance, a benefit for Rubin "Hurricane" Carter. Muhammad Ali appears to speak and accept a phone call from Carter, transmitted live from his prison cell in Trenton, New Jersey. The crowd goes wild.

DAVID GAHR

Right: On the Rolling Thunder tour, with Roger McGuinn, Joni Mitchell, Richie Havens and Joan Baez

_1976._ Columbia releases an album recorded live during the Rolling Thunder Revue, called _Hard Rain_....

. . . and is our purpose not the same
on this earth?
To love and follow His direction . . .
Time is an ocean but it ends at
the shore.
You may not see me Tomorrow.

Listen, we can work it out. Let's rise above these divisive quarrels and realize our real mutual self-interest. And with that solemn plea Dylan rings down the curtain for act one, on the first side of this album.

"Joey" opens the second side of this record, as did "Hurricane" on the first, with another heroic tribute to another odd Dylan hero—this time a colorful New York gangster who's just been gunned down during dinner with his family in a clam bar not far from where Dylan has lived and hung out for years. Joey Gallo was an authentic outlaw, "always on the outside of whatever side there was . . . caught between the mob and the men in blue." He had a "mad dog" reputation for being a real crazy. He read Nietzsche and Reich for ten years in Attica. A white friend of the black man, he was a protector of children, a Robin Hood thug captured by Dylan in the vernacular of the streets:

> I pray we realize soon we are all of one soul.
> —Bob Dylan

Prayer at Newport Beach, Rhode Island, during Rolling Thunder tour

WIDE WORLD PHOTOS

> **Dylan has invented himself. He's made himself up from scratch. That is, from the things he had around him and inside him. Dylan is an invention of his own mind. The point isn't to figure him out but to take him in. He gets into you anyway, so why not just take him in? He's not the first one to have invented himself, but he's the first one to have invented Dylan. What happens when someone invents something outside himself like an airplane or a freight train? . . . it's taken in by the people and changes their lives in the process. They don't stand around trying to figure out what it isn't, forever. They use it as a means to adventure. —Sam Shepard**

In *Rolling Thunder Logbook,* © 1977 by Sam Shepard

Joey, Joey
King of the streets, child of clay
Joey, Joey
What made them want to come and
blow you away?

Some thought this a strange choice of heroes, but Joey Gallo *was* really beloved among some, and—because he was a rebel gangster with personal style, iconoclastic morality, and a tragic end—it's logical for Dylan to deliver this euology. He might even have gone to the funeral.

"Romance in Durango" shifts gears completely. We're back to love and adventure with a Mexican setting. Dylan's written many songs with a Latin flavor, but this is probably the best. He even sings in Spanish, beautifully. It's an idyllic vision of Mexico, an American view of Mexico from a Jewish fellow who must have loved the Cisco Kid and *Treasure of Sierra Madre* and *Vera Cruz,* Rita Hayworth and Marlon Brando as Emiliano Zapata. The song is like a short film, in fact, with Dylan fleeing on horseback with a beautiful senorita, selling his guitar for a place to hide, on the lam, an outlaw, shot at the end. What an actor!

"Black Diamond Bay" could be a film, too, but the director would have to be Michelangelo Antonioni. This is a complex, surrealistic ballad with a wonderful batch of characters right out of a novel by Joseph Conrad: a mysterious lady, the Greek, the soldier, the desk clerk, and the dealer—all entwined together in some faraway hotel, waiting to be blown away by an earthquake by the bay. Meanwhile Dylan's sitting in his living room at the last verse, watching the whole yarn on television with a beer in his hand, hearing the news ("Oh, boy . . .") about this far gone disaster, then matter-of-factly dismissing it:

Seems like every time you turn around
There's another hard luck
Story that you're gonna hear
And there's really nothin'
Anyone can say
And I never did plan to go any way
To Black Diamond Bay.

First he sucks us into caring about these misfits, then he distances both himself and us. Ironically. It's just a story, folks, remember that? But what if we're in it?

Dylan pulls out all the stops on the last cut of the album, "Sara." On an album of strong, powerful material, this song is the strongest and most powerful. More powerful even than

> Music *is* truthful. Everything's okay, you put on a record, someone's playing an instrument—that changes the vibes. Music attracts the angels in the universe. A group of angels sitting at a table are going to be attracted by that. . . . —Bob Dylan

To Jonathan Cott in The *Rolling Stone* Interview, © 1978 by Straight Arrow Publishers, Inc.

"Oh, Sister" because of its naked emotion, it's coming right out and letting us know exactly what he's feeling about the lover he's losing. There's nothing hidden in this song, no symbolism, no metaphors. It's like reading someone's private letters or a secret diary. Dylan uses the real names, talks about the children, recollects the song he wrote for her . . . and he can't understand, can't accept that she's *changed her mind.* It's reminiscent of the hotel scene in *The Great Gatsby* when Tom tries to persuade Daisy to remember their love and stay with him. There's nothing left out, just listen to these lines:

Sara, Sara
Sweet virgin angel, sweet love of my life
Sara, Sara
Radiant jewel, mystical wife . . .
Lovin' you is the one thing I'll never regret . . . .
Beautiful lady, so dear to my heart . . .
You must forgive me my unworthiness . . . .

But unlike Tom, Dylan doesn't seem to be getting his wife back, nor does he appear to have any real confidence that they'll ever reunite, as the song ends in a prayer and a poignant, very painful, long, long, long held last note:

Sara, oh, Sara
Don't ever leave me, don't ever goooo . . . .

And she's gone. We know it. The one he wrote "Sad-Eyed Lady of the Lowlands" for. Gone for good.

Desire is an album by a mature artist at the height of his powers. Undiminished. Stronger than ever. Everything about this album is polished to a new level of perfection: the cover art, the myriad graphic details, each hinting, each revealing glimpses of the songs within; Dylan's own preamble, which summarizes the entire album's content in twenty-one pithy lines; the lengthier tribute by Allen Ginsberg; the excellent personnel, including good technicians in the studio, great musicians on accompaniment and exceptional back-up vocalists. It's a *tour de force*: two public songs ("Hurricane" and "Joey"), some far-out films and novellas in ballad form ("Isis," "Mozambique," "Romance in Durango," "Black Diamond Bay"), and three devastating summations on the death of love between man and woman ("One More Cup of Coffee," "Oh, Sister," "Sara")—love songs that show us his mortal wounds.

Mortal but not fatal. Dylan has survived and understood and WRITTEN these songs, after all. Tender and Jewish, macho and Mexican, no matter what disguise he assumes, the raw open heart comes through, and he *knows* it, he *shows* it, he's brave enough to get it all down.

Hard Rain

Columbia PC 34349. Produced by Don DeVito and Bob Dylan. Released 1976. Maggie's Farm, One Too Many Mornings, Stuck Inside of Mobile with the Memphis Blues Again (*all by Bob Dylan*), Oh, Sister (*B. Dylan, J. Levy*), Lay, Lady, Lay (*B. Dylan*); Shelter from the Storm, You're a Big Girl Now, I Threw It All Away, Idiot Wind (*all by Bob Dylan*).

JOSEPH SIA

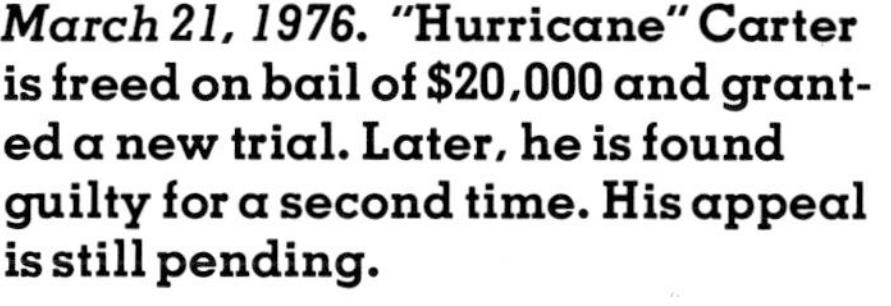

***March 21, 1976.* "Hurricane" Carter is freed on bail of $20,000 and granted a new trial. Later, he is found guilty for a second time. His appeal is still pending.**

Dylan, meanwhile, has moved to Malibu, on the Pacific Coast Highway near Los Angeles, where he begins to construct an enormous house by the beach. Starting with a simple plan, the building grows and grows into a dome-topped mansion that is alleged to cost over one million dollars.

OVERLEAF: JOSEPH SIA

NEAL PRESTON/MIRAGE

Finale

WIDE WORLD PHOTOS

"My new songs are new for me, and they accomplish what I wanted to accomplish when I started thinking about them. Very seldom do you finish something and then abandon it, and very seldom do you abandon something with the attitude that you've gotten what you started out to get. Usually you think, well, it's too big, you get wasted along the way someplace, and it just trails off . . . and what you've got is what you've got and you do the best with it. But very seldom do you ever come out with what you put in. And I think I've done that now for the first time since I was writing two songs a day way back when. . . ." —Bob Dylan

To Jonathan Cott in The *Rolling Stone* Interview, © 1978 by Straight Arrow Publishers, Inc.

"Art is the perpetual motion of illusion. The highest purpose of art is to inspire. What else can you do? What else can you do for anyone but inspire them?" —Bob Dylan

To Jonathan Cott in The *Rolling Stone* Interview, © 1978 by Straight Arrow Publishers, Inc.

"I am interested in all aspects of life. Revelations and realizations. Lucid thought that can be translated into songs, analogies, new information. I am better at it now, not really written anything to make me stop writing. Like, I haven't come to the place that Rimbaud came to when he decided to stop writing and run guns in Africa."—Bob Dylan

To Ron Rosenbaum, © 1978 by *Playboy*

NEAL PRESTON/MIRAGE

February 1977. Bob and Sara Dylan separate. Dylan has chronicled the rise and fall of their relationship from "Sad-Eyed Lady of the Lowlands" through "Lay, Lady, Lay" to the complex difficulties of _Blood on the Tracks_ and _Desire_.

June 1977. Bob and Sara Dylan are divorced after thirteen years of marriage. Sara Dylan retains legal custody of their four children, Jesse, Anna, Samuel, and Jakos.

Thanksgiving, 1977. Dylan appears at The Band's farewell concert in San Francisco, "The Last Waltz." Martin Scorcese's film of the event appeared six months later.

BOB DYLAN
STREET-LEGAL

Street-Legal

Columbia JC 35453; Captain in Charge: Don De Vito; Released June 1978. Changing of the Guards; New Pony; No Time to Think; Baby Stop Crying; Is Your Love in Vain?; Senor (Tales of Yankee Power); True Love Tends to Forget; We Better Talk This Over; Where Are You Tonight? (Journey through Dark Heat). *All songs written by Bob Dylan.*

"What a sexy photograph!" a friend of ours said as she saw the front cover of the latest Bob Dylan album. And she's right. There he is, peeking out of a funky doorway, hand on his hips, his wiry body leaning out and looking around the corner, his bony shoulders straining taut against a blue work shirt. He looks tough and solid and ready and sexy. Alone, too. On his own again. And that's pretty much what his album is all about.

There's something very sober about the songs on this album. They're solid rhythmically, with good percussion from Ian Wallace and Bobbye Hall, keyboard by Alan Pasqua, some solid tenor and soprano saxaphone playing by Steve Douglas and background vocals in a black, rock and gospel style by Carolyn Dennis, Jo Ann Harris and Helena Springs—mostly new musicians that he's never recorded with before—plus some rhythm guitar and back-up vocalizing by Steven Soles. Despite their slick arrangements and punchy, driving rhythms, these songs sound quite somber and flat. The melodies are largely monotonous and Dylan's voice sounds hoarse and strained. His vocal track is often nearly drowned out by the instrumentals and background vocals. The overall effect is of someone kind of grim and depressed, forcing these songs out with a fatalistic attitude like: well here's the way it is for me now, not so hot, but still plugging.

You can hardly hear what Dylan's saying on the first cut, "Changing of the Guards," the scratchy, high-straining vocal track is so nearly drowned out by the powerful organ and sax and black-girl background. A big muddy song, a long symbolic, surrealistic narrative in the traditions of his apocalyptic visions from the "Times They Are A-Changin" period. Musically, the mood is dominated by a declining chord progression, a dirge-like descending pattern that reappears in several songs that follow.

"New Pony" is the best vocal on the album and has the most energy. It's a very funky, sexy blues about a man who had one Pony who's name was Lucifer who "broke her leg and needed shotting . . . I swear it hurts me more than it could have her . . ." Dauntless, our singer finds a new pony who can do the "fox-trot, low bear pace . . ." Backed by a raunchy lead guitar and sax, Dylan tells her to

Come over here, pony, I want to climb on top of you!

He's tough; he's dirty; he's a little cynical, too, having disposed of one filly and quick to mount another.

"No Time to Think" is a long, ironic sermon, accompanied by a beautiful violin duet between didactic verses documenting Dylan's familiar struggle between the pressures of external society, its expectations and demands, and his internal vision and drive. Throughout the verses, he and his back-up vocalists list a series of philosophical abstractions to grope with:

Loneliness . . . tenderness . . . high society . . . variety . . .

January 1978. Dylan releases a four-hour feature film he has made in 1975-1976 during the Rolling Thunder Revue called *Renaldo and Clara*. In this first totally-controlled, self-made film Dylan has refused to compromise: rather than allow a studio to cut the footage in half for commercial distribution, he forms his own company and spends over $1.5 million to produce and edit and market the film exactly the way he wants it.

***Renaldo and Clara* includes some incredible performance footage: intense, close shots of Dylan in white face spitting and barking out twenty-two of his classics with demonic power — songs we know in a way we've never known them before. Much of the film, however, consists of improvised semiautobiographical scenes staged with Dylan, his wife Sara, and Joan Baez in a series of ironic, playful scenes which mirror their real-life relationships. At one point Dylan asks Sara in Ms. Baez's presence, "Do you mean, do I love her like I love you?"**

February 1978. Dylan launches his first tour of Japan, which includes eight concerts in Tokyo and three in Osaka.

Renaldo and Clara opens to terrible reviews. Dylan is attacked in all the major media for insufferable egomania, arrogance, and self-indulgence. Dauntless, he defends the film in a series of painful interviews, and later cuts it down to a 90-minute movie.

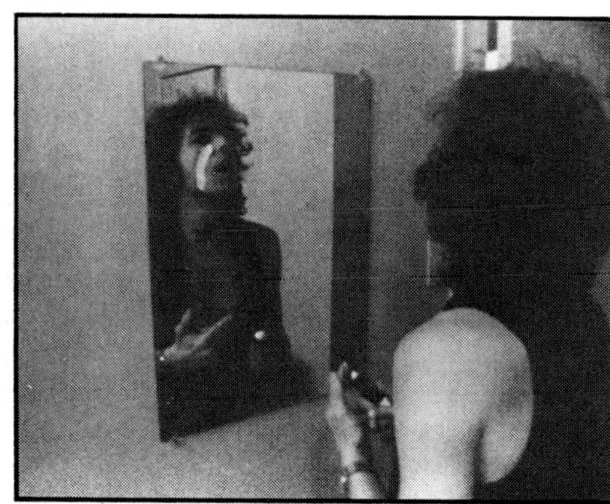

A Selected Bibliography

Dylan, Bob, 1976. *The Songs of Bob Dylan: From 1966 Through 1975.* Alfred A. Knopf, New York.

Dylan, Bob, 1973. *Writings and Drawings.* Alfred A. Knopf, New York.

McGregor, Craig, Editor, 1972. *Bob Dylan: A Retrospective.* William Morrow, New York.

Pickering, Stephen, 1975. *Bob Dylan Approximately: A Midrash.* David McKay, New York.

Rolling Stone, 1974. *Knockin' On Dylan's Door.* Pocket Books, New York.

Scaduto, Anthony, 1973. *Dylan: An Intimate Biography.* Grosset & Dunlap. New York.

Shepard, Sam, 1977. *Rolling Thunder Logbook.* A Richard Seaver Book. Viking. New York.

Memory . . . ecstasy . . . tyranny . . .
hypocrisy . . .
Paradise . . . sacrifice . . . mortality . . .
reality . . .
Equality . . . liberty . . . humility . . .
simplicity . . .
Socialism . . . hypnotism . . . patriotism . . . materialism . . .

There's also some terrific saxaphone playing by Steve Douglas in "Baby Stop Crying," a somewhat livelier number wherein Dylan consoles a woman who loves someone else. He's ready to get his pistol but she's still madly in love. This may be the first love song Dylan's written where even though the woman is "back where you belong," she still pines for someone else, not him. Again, there's that recurring musical descent, like a ship sinking slowly in the drink.

In the most personal and revealing song on this album, "Is Your Love in Vain", Dylan speaks from his heart, eloquently and with powerful effect:

Do you love me, or are you just extending good will
Do you need me half as bad as you say, or are you just feeling guilt?
I've been burned before and I know the score, so you won't hear me complain
Will I be able to count on you . . .
or is you love in vain.

Sad, chastened, the pain of his recent, disruptive divorce is plainly revealed in this moving lyric:

Are you so fast that you cannot see that I must have solitude
When I am in the darkness why do you intrude . . .
Well I've been to the mountain, and I've been in the wind
I've been in and out of happiness . . .
Do you understand my pain, are you willing to risk it all
Or is your love in vain.

The song may provide the key to Dylan's mood throughout the album. Basically, he's looking for love. Warily. Needy but cautious. He's back where he started from in so many ways: the world is still bearing in on him, it's hard for any of us to understand the pressure. Love is available but he's withdrawn and suspicious, still wounded from big ups and bad downs of his past.

"Senor (Tales of Yankee Power)" opens the second side with a mini-drama reminiscent of the songs Dylan wrote with Jacques Levy for *Desire.* In this ballad, the singer seems to be under the heel of both a lost love and an oppressive political regime. The story works on two levels: he's looking for his woman; he's trying to break out of some prison-like existence:

The last thing I remember before I stripped and kneeled
Was a train load of fools brought down in a magnetic field
A gypsy with a broken flag and a flashing ring
He's saying, "Son, this ain't a dream no more, it's the real thing . . ."

Is he waiting to be shot? Certainly there's a strong sense of doom in this song sung from under some rock, particularly as he concludes, "I'm ready when you are, Senor." Yankee Power. Oppression. A metaphor for the sense of loss and the pressure from without that Dylan seems to be expressing continuously in each of these numbers. Again, the saxaphone is marvelous and Dylan does muster a somewhat less scratchy and deeper voice on this track.

"True Love Tends to Forget" is another sad, post-separation song of lost love:

I'm getting weary looking in my lady's eyes
When she's near me she's so hard to recognize
When I finally realize . . . there's no room for me there.
True love tends to forget . . .

"We Better Talk this Over" is a little faster, with an upbeat country and western style but it, too, has a somewhat cynical attitude toward a potential love affair that Dylan surmises isn't likely to work.

Finally, "Where Are You Tonight" concludes this album with another depressing anthem about a woman he longs to touch. The music is sad as hell; the words are candid:

In that last hour of need, we entirely agreed
Sacrifice was the code of the road . . .

And Dylan, the Gemini, tells us how:

I fought with my twin. That enemy within.
'Til both of us fell by the way . . .

Despite the cooking instrumental backing, we leave Dylan there, fallen.

Street-Legal, the last album we are able to include, has been released during a burst of activity from Dylan in the wake of his film *Renaldo and Clara.* Dylan's tour of Japan and Australia was a resounding success. Tickets for his appearances in England during the spring of 1978 sold out within hours. Another major tour of the United States is being planned for this coming fall. It's clear that Dylan is working hard, producing a lot of new music, new albums, perhaps ultimately even another new film.

So the mood of *Street-Legal*—hard, strained, deliberate, depressing—may be as ephemeral as many others he has passed through. We hope for something more uplifting, more optimistic, more loving . . . and in the meantime we remain fascinated and attentive.

> "If a mystery is solved, the case is dropped. In this case, in the case of Dylan, the mystery is never solved, so the case keeps on. It keeps coming up again. Over and over the years. Who is this character anyway? — Sam Shepard"

In *Rolling Thunder Logbook,* © 1977 by Sam Sheppard

> "The Seventies I see as a period of reconstruction after the Sixties, that's all. That's why people say: well, it's boring, nothing's really happening, and that's because wounds are healing. By the Eighties, anyone who's going to be doing anything will have his or her cards showing. You won't be able to get back in the game in the Eighties. — Bob Dylan"

To Jonathan Cott in *Rolling Stone* Interview, © 1978 by Straight Arrow Publishers, Inc.

$8.95

"The longer you live, the better you get..."

—Bob Dylan

Bob Dylan has been called a poet, a prophet, a mystic Jewish *rebbe*. But he remains first and foremost a musician: a song writer and performing artist of staggering genius and enormous influence throughout the world. *Bob Dylan: The Illustrated Record* chronicles the full sweep of Dylan's life and career in music — and by so doing also presents a striking narration of a period in history when much of what is occurring on the cultural, political and psycho-personal landscape has been embodied and expressed through popular music and especially, Bob Dylan's music. ¶*Bob Dylan: The Illustrated Record* provides a wealth of important research, biographical material, musical exegesis/and critical evaluation: it is a thorough and comprehensive compendium of facts, quotations, significant events, memorabilia—all handsomely designed and profusely illustrated with album sleeves and over one hundred photographs, many never seen before. Spanning nearly twenty years, *Bob Dylan: The Illustrated Record* is a rich and fascinating documentary of a truly extraordinary phenomenon.

Photographs, clockwise from top left: © 1978, Rex Features, Chuck Krall, Rex Features, Jim Marshall, Columbia Records, and Rex Features.

ISBN O 517 53355 3